P9-APO-661

Catch!

Catch!

A Fishmonger's Guide to Greatness

by Cyndi Crother and
the crew of World Famous
Pike Place Fish

BK

BERRETT-KOEHLER PUBLISHERS, INC.
San Francisco

Copyright © 2004 by Cyndi Crother and Fish Boys LLC

All rights reserved. No part of this publication may be reproduced, distributed, or transmitted in any form or by any means, including photocopying, recording, or other electronic or mechanical methods, without the prior written permission of the publisher, except in the case of brief quotations embodied in critical reviews and certain other noncommercial uses permitted by copyright law. For permission requests, write to the publisher, addressed "Attention: Permissions Coordinator," at the address below.

Berrett-Koehler Publishers, Inc.

235 Montgomery Street, Suite 650, San Francisco, CA 94104-2916

Tel: (415) 288-0260   Fax: (415) 362-2512   www.bkconnection.com

Ordering Information

Quantity sales. Special discounts are available on quantity purchases by corporations, associations, and others. For details, contact the "Special Sales Department" at the Berrett-Koehler address above.

Individual sales. Berrett-Koehler publications are available through most bookstores. They can also be ordered direct from Berrett-Koehler: Tel: (800) 929-2929; Fax: (802) 864-7626; www.bkconnection.com

Orders for college textbook/course adoption use. Please contact Berrett-Koehler: Tel: (800) 929-2929; Fax: (802) 864-7626;

Orders by U.S. trade bookstores and wholesalers. Please contact Publishers Group West, 1700 Fourth Street, Berkeley, CA 94710. Tel: (510) 528-1444; Fax (510) 528-3444.

Berrett-Koehler and the BK logo are registered trademarks of Berrett-Koehler Publishers, Inc.

Printed in the United States of America

Berrett-Koehler books are printed on long-lasting acid-free paper. When it is available, we choose paper that has been manufactured by environmentally responsible processes. These may include using trees grown in sustainable forests, incorporating recycled paper, minimizing chlorine in bleaching, or recycling the energy produced at the paper mill.

LIBRARY OF CONGRESS CATALOGING-IN-PUBLICATION DATA

Crother, Cyndi, 1970–

Catch!: a fishmonger's guide to greatness / by Cyndi Crother and the crew of World Famous Pike Place Fish.

   p. cm.

Includes index.

ISBN 1-57675-254-2 (alk. pap.)

ISBN 1-57675-323-9 (pbk.)

1. World Famous Pike Place Fish (Seattle, Wash.). 2. Fish trade—Washington (State)—Seattle. 3. Success in business. 4. Management—Case studies. 5. Success —Psychological aspects. 6. Self-realization. I. Title: Fishmonger's guide to greatness. II. World Famous Pike Place Fish (Seattle, Wash.) III. Title.

HD9459.W67C76 2003

650.1—DC22   2003057803

First Edition

09 08 07 06 05   10 9 8 7 6 5

Copyediting: Todd A. Manza. Book design: Valerie Brewster, Scribe Typography

Contents

Preface

The World Famous Pike Place Fish Market is located in the Pike Place Public Market in Seattle, Washington. When John Yokoyama (Johnny) purchased the fish market in 1965, it was nothing like it is today. In the beginning, it was pretty ordinary and operated just as one would expect any fish market to operate. Although it is still one of four fish markets at the Pike Place Public Market, there is nothing ordinary about World Famous Pike Place Fish.

World Famous Pike Place Fish is now a destination point for visitors to Seattle. Even people unfamiliar with Pike Place Fish by name usually recognize it as the place that throws fish when customers make a purchase. Often they have seen the fish market on NBC's *Frasier* or MTV's *The Real World*, on *Emeril Live* or *Wheel of Fortune,* or in the movie *Free Willie.* Pike Place Fish has also been publicized in any number of magazines and newspapers, including *Fast Company* and the *Toronto Star,* and they hold a *Guinness* world record for the most fish thrown in a minute!

ChartHouse Learning Corporation produced two award-winning corporate training films about the market, *Fish!* and *Fish! Sticks,* and published *Fish!,* a book that made the *Wall Street Journal* and *New York Times* bestseller lists, and lists in Japan and Germany. In March 2001, CNN identified the World Famous Pike Place Fish Market as "the most fun place to work" in the United States.

Hardly what one would expect from a bunch of fishmongers, but these are no ordinary fishmongers.

These days, Pike Place Fish and their partner biz-FUTURES Consulting are working together to share their insights with organizations both domestically and internationally. Johnny, Jim Bergquist, and a handful of fishmongers travel to organizations and conferences to throw fish, create a lot of excitement, and generate interest in a more powerful way of doing business and living life. Most importantly, they make a difference for people.

Pike Place Fish employs fifteen to seventeen fishmongers, depending on seasonal activity. The term *fishmonger* is a fifteenth-century term meaning "fish dealer." On any given day, six to nine fishmongers sell fish at the Market. Pike Place Fish is open for business every day of the year — twelve hours a day Monday through Saturday, and ten hours on Sunday. While they are best known for the energy and excitement they generate at the Market, they are less known for their unprecedented financial results. In the past seventeen years, Pike Place Fish's cost of doing business has dropped nearly twenty-five percent, revenues have quadrupled, and profits have increased tenfold!

I teach quality assurance and corporate training in the Industrial Technology Department at California Polytechnic State University in San Luis Obispo, California, and I learned about Pike Place Fish at a leadership conference in fall 2001. At first, I thought Pike Place Fish might be offering a new organizational quality initiative, and I wanted more information, to see if I should incorporate their concepts into my classes.

The hype surrounding Pike Place Fish intrigued me. It was unclear why a little fish market in Seattle was getting so much acclaim from corporations large and small in virtually every sector imaginable. I even found several companies in San Luis Obispo talking about Pike Place Fish, including the local feed store where I buy supplies for my horse. It appeared everyone was interested in Pike Place Fish!

My curiosity turned into a desire to tell their story. At the time, I wasn't sure how this might come about, but I felt strongly that people everywhere could benefit from learning more about the guiding principles of Pike Place Fish. It is my intention to make a difference in people's lives, and I was amazed to find a business that held many beliefs similar to my own. It seemed there was much to be learned behind the scenes at this little fish market, so I contacted the owner of Pike Place Fish and proposed sharing the organization's underlying beliefs and guiding principles with the rest of the world.

I first met the fishmongers in February 2002, and I visited them several times throughout the year while continuing to teach at Cal Poly. During my visits I worked at the Market, set up the smoked salmon and box displays, and helped put things away at night. I learned the physical aspects of the job as well as the fishmongers' jargon and the mental aspects of their work. I spent a lot of time talking to the guys — sometimes in formal interview settings, and sometimes just in casual conversations. I was even fortunate enough to be hit in the head by a flying crab and locked in the cooler on the same day—it was quite an experience!

One of the biggest and most important life lessons I learned from the fishmongers is that I am responsible for what I experience in my life and for whatever future I cause to happen in my life. The fishmongers call that idea "It's all over here"—each person is solely responsible for his or her thoughts, feelings, emotions, decisions, actions... everything. Virtually every story in *Catch!* illustrates the guiding principle at Pike Place Fish: You are responsible for your life.

For example, if I am upset because I have to stand in a long line at the grocery store, I am not upset at the line or the people in line. I am upset because I am choosing to be upset; chances are, standing in line does not match my expectation of going to the grocery store. The idea is that nothing outside of yourself makes you happy or sad—it's all within you; hence, "It's all over here."

Catch! is the story behind the hype, and it relates the real experiences of the fishmongers who work at Pike Place Fish. At times, the language they use may seem a bit awkward because they use many catchphrases (no pun intended) with one another, at work and in their personal lives. However, it's not the specific language they use that makes the stories so powerful. Rather, the language is simply a reflection of their underlying guiding principles. Through their stories, you will experience their guiding principles and their own personal transformations, and if the fishmongers can do it, so can you. How did they do it? Welcome to their stories...

The first chapter tells you about World Famous Pike Place Fish. It introduces you to the fishmongers, gives you a glimpse into a normal day at the Market, and provides insights into the language – and into the thinking behind the language. The second chapter reveals the main underlying tenets that allow effective use of the guiding principles. Chapter 3 discusses the notions of intention and commitment, because the remaining chapters derive from one's clear understanding of his or her intention and commitment.

Once you find your intention and are committed to making it happen, your eyes will be open to new and exciting opportunities, as revealed in Chapter 4. In Chapter 5, you will see how these new opportunities – and how you think about these opportunities – begin to shape your new reality. You will see the importance of language as a tool in this shaping and in connecting to other human beings.

Once you have these new ideas under your belt, Chapter 6 gives a specific application of them and invites you to recognize conflict and problems as a good thing, since creative conflict leads to many opportunities for growth and development.

Finally, all of the guiding principles are integrated in Chapter 7, giving you the tools to access a more effective and meaningful way of living and working. Through their stories, you will learn how all members of one company are nurturing and sustaining a healthy work environment. I hope you will be inspired to more fully actualize these concepts in your life and to really catch *Catch!*

Cyndi Crother
August 2003

Acknowledgments

This book would not have been possible without the contributions of many delightful people from many different parts of the world. Since commencing this project, I have met many individuals who have added important dimensions to my understanding of life, many of whom I remain in close contact with today. While there are too many to mention here, I thank all of you for your kindness.

The crew and I thank World Famous Pike Place Fish owner Johnny Yokoyama and bizFUTURES consultant Jim Bergquist for the opportunity to share these stories and guiding principles with the world.

This book really would not have been possible without the entire staff at Berrett-Koehler Publishing. They have been an utter pleasure to work with. I owe special thanks to Publisher Steve Piersanti for having faith in my abilities as an author, for teaching me about the world of publishing, and for creative inspiration. I am particularly indebted to Managing Editor Jeevan Sivasubramaniam for taking a risk, for all of his mentoring, and for becoming a great friend along the way.

A special thanks is in order for the many fantastic reviewers who shaped this work. I owe debts of gratitude to Tiffiny Aasen, Russell Ackoff, Gary Anderson, Sandy Chase, Cheryl Crother (my mom), Mike Crowley, Marcia Daszko, Amie Devero, Kathleen Epperson, Theresa Frappia, Jennee La Lanne, Chris Lee, Carol P. McCoy, Connie McNoble,

Beverly Murray-Scherf, Sarah Pahlow, Jade Stone, Mavis Wilson, and Don Yates. For their assistance with endorsements, I wish to thank Graham Gawne, Michael Kennedy, Nancy Kent, Lois Mitchell, and Ron Trego. I thank Bill Bellows for my first opportunity to introduce the book to the public. For his creative nature, and for taking most of the photographs found throughout the book, I am most grateful to and thank my dad, Larry Crother.

I also wish to express my deepest appreciation to the students of the Industrial Technology Department at California Polytechnic University, San Luis Obispo for their excitement about this adventure, as well as my colleagues Fred Abitia, Larry Gay, Rod Hoadley, Roger Keep, Dave Kimble, Lezlie Labhard, Al Lipper, Tony Randazzo, Lee Sneller, and Jeannie Souza. Your encouragement has been invaluable, and you have kept my spirit smiling.

1 A Day in the Life of World Famous Pike Place Fish

Cast of Characters

Throughout this book, you will be reading stories from each of the fishmongers, so it might help to know a little bit about them. **Johnny Yokoyama** purchased Pike Place Fish in 1965 and used to work at the Market with the guys. These days the fishmongers pretty much keep the fish flying on their own; however, Johnny remains actively involved in coaching the crew and in leading them into an exciting and inspiring future.

Dicky Yokoyama, Johnny's brother, started working at Pike Place Fish over twenty years ago and is presently one of the managers. **Samuel "Sammy" Samson** is the other manager, but you usually can't see him because he's moving so darn fast! **Keith Bish,** otherwise known as "Bear," was the driver and utility person for years; now you can find him working at the king salmon display. **Justin Hall** has been working at Pike Place Fish since he was thirteen

Dicky Yokoyama

years old. He has been there for thirteen years, and his claim to fame is being in the *Guinness Book of World Records* for the most fish thrown in a minute.

Jaison Scott was practically born at the Market, and

Keith Bish (aka Bear)

Justin Hall

Samuel "Sammy" Samson

he has worked at Pike Place Fish for seven years. He is well known as an outstanding drummer for Severhead, a hard-driving Seattle band. **Darren Kilian** has been with Pike Place Fish for five years; he can usually be found at the

Jaison Scott

Darren Kilian

Dan Bugge (aka Bugge)   *Chris Bell*

computer near the clam and mussel displays, putting together many of the Internet orders. **Dan Bugge,** known to everyone by just his last name, has been with Pike Place Fish for three years. He is best known for throwing a fish into a baby carriage — with the baby still in it! Don't worry; the baby was okay, if a bit startled.

Chris Bell currently is the utility person and driver. Every day he picks up the freshest fish available to mankind and keeps the rhythm going by making sure

Andy Frigulietti   *Erik Espinoza*

Ryan Dehn (aka Bison)   *Anders Miller*

everything is well stocked. **Andy Frigulietti** came to Seattle from Boston and has worked with Pike Place Fish for nearly four years. He works in front of the crab and lobster displays with **Erik Espinoza,** who has worked at the Market for about two years. Erik has had the opportunity to travel to some interesting vacation destinations.

   Ryan Dehn, also known as **"Bison,"** has worked on and off with Pike Place Fish for about three years. Hard to track down, Bison's always on the go and keeps all the displays

Jeremy Ridgway   *Russell Price*

Ben Bish

Matt Lewis

well stocked. **Anders Miller** has been with Pike Place Fish for about three years and spends most of his time behind the counter (also known as "up on top"), catching and filleting the fish thrown his way. He also delivers orders to the hotels after the shop closes in the evening. Usually behind the counter with Anders is **Jeremy Ridgway**, a self-proclaimed expert-in-training who has been with Pike Place Fish for about one year.

When he's not cruising around Seattle on his Harley, **Russell Price** works in front of the king salmon or crab displays and has been aboard for three years. **Ben Bish,** Bear's son, has been working part-time at Pike Place Fish since he was fifteen years old. He also generally works out in front, by the crab and shellfish displays or by the king salmon display.

Matt Lewis, Doug Strauss, Dave Brooks, and **Ryan Kimura** also worked at Pike Place Fish while I was compiling the stories for the book. Matt and Dave are now attending college, Doug teaches high school locally, and Ryan moved to Las Vegas for another job opportunity.

Each of them visits Pike Place Fish regularly, so you might see them at the Market as well.

One thing to note is that each of the fishmongers is responsible for being able to do anything that is required — cross training at its finest! They each work up on top, answer the phones, work out in front, put together shipping orders, make deliveries — everything.

Other contributing members of the cast are longtime consultant **Jim Bergquist** and his team, who help facilitate the process of creating goals and solving problems at Pike Place Fish.

Catch! of the Day

If you have not had the opportunity to visit Pike Place Fish, it might be helpful to know what a normal day looks like. Every day except Sunday begins at 6:30 A.M. (Sunday begins at 7:00 A.M.), when the fishmongers get into a huddle to discuss the goals for the day. They talk about how much inventory of each type of fish they have on hand and about what they want to accomplish on that day. The huddle ends with a loud, ceremonial "Aayyyyeeee!"

After the huddle, each fishmonger sets up a different seafood display, called a "show." On a typical day, the shows include smoked, boxed, and king salmon, shellfish and crab, parrot fish and other exotic-looking fish, monkfish, clams and mussels, and oysters. While some of the fishmongers set up the displays in front of the counter, other fishmongers work behind the counter, cutting up the fillets and steaks for display behind the glass.

Entrance to Pike Place Public Market with World Famous Pike Place Fish on the left

Once everything is set up, the fishmongers hose down the walkways, clean the display case glass, and hang labels to identify the different types of fish. Many of the fillets and steaks look quite similar, and it takes a keen eye to distinguish between them. All the while, early-bird customers are making purchases. In addition to the fish products, customers buy "World Famous Pike Place Fish" T-shirts, sweatshirts, hats, and other goodies. As the day unfolds, increasing numbers of visitors and customers come to the Market, creating a lot of activity. The fishmongers move all day, taking orders off the phone and the Internet and shipping fish to every imaginable distant corner of the world.

If you want to see the action from your home, check out the Pike Place Fish website and select *webcam*. One of the things you will see is that any time a customer places an order, the fishmonger serving him or her literally throws the fish about ten to fifteen feet to another fishmonger, who catches it while standing behind the counter. There is not a lot of room for error, but the fishmongers have become quite skilled at throwing crab, salmon, and even bags of clams. It is a well-synchronized process, and no one throws a fish until the fishmonger taking the order calls out the specific order to the others. Once the order is yelled to the crew, the crew responds by repeating the order aloud. Then the fish fly! Because of their communication system, it is rare to see the fishmongers make a mistake.

Originally, the crew threw fish in order to avoid walking all the way to the counter to weigh a customer's order. However, customers and visitors got such a kick out of seeing fish fly that it has become a part of Pike Place Fish's culture. Sometimes customers even get in on the action, and while visiting the Market you might see someone try their hand at catching a flying fish. This usually gets many laughs from the watching crowd—those fish can be slippery!

At 5:45 p.m., sharp, one of the fishmongers yells "five forty-five" to initiate the closing process. It takes approximately forty-five minutes to break down the displays and put away all the fish for the night. By 6:30, everything is stowed, and the crew gets into another huddle. They talk about how the day went in relation to the goals that were

Stocked displays at the Pike Place Fish stall

set in the morning huddle. They divide the tips they earned throughout the course of the day, and then they close shop. One of the fishmongers will then deliver orders to customers who are guests staying at the various local hotels.

The Map and the Territory

One thing that you may notice as you read through the fishmongers' stories is that sometimes their language seems a little odd. While the terms and jargon are catchy, the power of the stories does not come from the specific terms; it comes from the attitude and mental framework reflected in the terms. The language is simply a reflection of the concepts and underlying Pike Place Fish principles.

The relationship between the language and the principles is analogous to a map and the territory a map depicts. A map is not exactly what the actual territory looks like, but it is nonetheless a depiction of the characteristics of the territory. The map represents a tool to help you understand what you might expect in the actual territory. The same is true of the language the fishmongers use: the language is simply a tool to understand the guiding principles that make the fishmongers effective in their lives and at work.

Before we get started, Russell and Anders have the following introduction for you:

> Some of you may know who we are, and some of you may not. Whatever the case may be, we want to acknowledge you for supporting us and believing in what we stand for, for the commitment to yourself that led you to this book, and for your willingness to listen to some ideas that may be different from the ones you have now. We believe your willingness to be open to these ideas is the key to a future of infinite possibilities. Enjoy!

> *Russell and Anders*

Review of Chapter 1

✳ Organizational greatness starts with individual greatness.

✳ Pike Place Fish language is simply a tool to help you understand the underlying guiding principles shared in the fishmongers' stories.

✳ The intention of *Catch!* is to offer you the tools to put the fishmongers' beliefs into action and to become more effective in your life and work.

2 Ordinary to Great

It's All over Here

People from all over the world visit World Famous Pike Place Fish to be jazzed up and to see the fishmongers throw fish. People will watch for hours in all weather, frigid or sunny (yes, it does get sunny in Seattle!). The fish market is a dynamic and exciting environment to visit, and while it is easy to see the fun, it is not as easy to see the philosophies behind the fun — the set of beliefs that the fishmongers live by to make it happen.

The intention of *Catch!* is to show you the workings of an organization that is different than most. The best part is that the fishmongers are ordinary people living extra-ordinary lives. The fishmongers offer you examples of how to put their beliefs into action in your own life — to unleash your own potential for greatness. There is a path to greatness; however, each person experiences it differently. The catch is that *ordinary* happens, but *greatness* is generated.

Many people go through life *reacting* to circumstances and events rather than *creating* what happens. The vision of Pike Place Fish is to make a positive difference in people's lives. By sharing their stories and insights, we hope to help you come one step closer to achieving greatness in your life. It is not so much that you follow the fishmongers' process; rather, we want you to see that there is a place making a difference in the world, and that place is the World Famous Pike Place Fish Market.

There is an unspoken pattern within most of the stories — the underlying belief that "It's all over here." At Pike Place Fish, this simple statement refers to the principle that I am responsible for what I experience and how I react to what occurs in my life. The fishmongers' sense of responsibility for themselves and for others within their organization is demonstrated through their actions and language. Their stories reflect an underlying set of guiding questions, including:

* What is my intention?
* Are my behaviors aligned with my intention?
* Does what I am doing reflect my intention?
* What is the outcome that I am going to make happen?

The first story, told by Chris, not only reflects the pattern noted above but also depicts how ordinary happens and greatness is generated. Before working at Pike Place Fish, Chris worked at a customer service call center for a well-known phone company. At the time, he was unaware of the choices that could make his work and his life much more fulfilling. He had goals about what he wanted in life but he wasn't doing anything proactive to achieve them. He didn't feel like an integral part of a team at work, and more importantly, he didn't know that there was a possibility that it could be any different.

> Before working at Pike Place Fish, I was going through the motions of work, just letting life happen. Things would come up and I'd deal with them. I had a vision of being financially successful but I wasn't doing any of the footwork to make it happen, nor was I really committed to making it happen.

Chris did not think of his job at the call center as a career. He never felt ownership of what occurred at work. He worked on the phone with a caller, fixed the caller's problem, and away they went. In his mind, anyone could replace him at his computer, doing his duties.

> Since I've been working at Pike Place Fish, I've dedicated myself to the visions of "world famous" and making a difference in the world. I re-dedicate myself every day. Things still come up, but I've learned that I can choose to do a world famous job or just do it half-ass. I now know it's my choice. It feels like if I am not here, my contribution isn't either. While I

could have had the same experience at the call center, I just didn't know at the time that it was a possibility.

If I went back to the call center now, work would be a world of difference. Every customer would feel they just experienced the best customer service they'd ever had and would feel I took care of them effectively. They would know I genuinely cared about how they felt about my service. And I wouldn't just keep it to myself. I'd show other people on my team how to create relationships and treat people like people, rather than somebody at the other end of the phone.

My customer service ratings at the call center were high, and I felt like I did a good job. But knowing what I know now, I wouldn't just do a good job — I'd be doing a world-class job and getting everyone around me to be doing it, too.

Chris

From Human Doers to Human Beings

While selling fish is the primary focus of Pike Place Fish, it is only part of the equation. One guiding principle that makes Pike Place Fish so unique is the fishmongers' awareness of *doing* and *being*. It is ironic that we call ourselves human *beings*, because we tend to be far more concerned with what we are *doing*. As human doers go, we can do some pretty amazing things; however, the fishmongers realize that awareness of who they are being is just as important, if not more important, than an awareness of what they are doing.

Being is not exactly a new concept, but there seems to be a shift in thinking taking place; people are increasingly concerned with the quality of their life experience. It is important to realize that your experience and your achievements are the result of what you do, of your actions and behaviors. What you do results from your being, your essence, or what makes you uniquely *you*. The process is depicted in the following diagram:

Being ⟶ Doing ⟶ Having

Being includes your core beliefs or underlying assumptions. Your essence and underlying assumptions drive what you do. *Doing* refers to the act of performing your actions and your observable behaviors. Ultimately, who you are being and what you are doing leads to outcomes. *Having* reflects a natural occurrence, a result or consequence of one's attitudes, understanding, and behaviors.

So, what does this mean to the fishmongers?

The fishmongers have fun at Pike Place Fish, but the fun is not simply a result of throwing fish. They have fun at work because each fishmonger takes personal responsibility for the fulfillment of the Pike Place Fish vision of "world famous" and for making a positive difference in people's lives.

In the following story, Dicky recollects Pike Place Fish's process of transformation. Dicky has worked with many different fishmongers over twenty years, and he believes that the current crew's greatness is a result of an awareness of who they are being. He believes the first step to understanding *being* is to recognize one's intention.

> There was a lot more to our transformation to greatness than what we were doing. We used to be like most fish markets, but then we started having meetings in the back room. It didn't seem like a big deal at the time. We'd have beer, sit there for hours, and create financial goals for the month — after working all day. It was a start.

Pike Place Fish has always been good to customers, and quality has always been very important. There was a time when they made one thousand dollars a day and thought it was big bucks. Dicky really started noticing the changes at the fish market after they began having their meetings. Once their consultant joined them, the meetings became a powerful force for transformation to occur. Now Pike Place Fish makes twenty times that in a day, with fewer employees.

> We started with discussing ideas of intention, commitment, and integrity, and new possibilities came into the picture. Recognizing our intention changed who we were being as individuals and who we were as a group. It was all here, and with my brother Johnny's lead,

everything started to transform. We started
having meetings every other week, and the
whole company started to transform.

Dicky

The crew of Pike Place Fish believes transformation
from ordinary to great comes from being great in all that
you do. It involves knowing your intention and exploring
the beliefs by which you live. It might be easy to perform
one act of greatness (similar to an act of kindness), but it
is another story to be great in all that you do. To truly be
great is a way of life — it becomes *you.*

At Pike Place Fish, the fishmongers are aware of and
take responsibility for who they are being and what they
are doing, which is demonstrated in their thinking, their
language, and their actions with one another and with
customers. The fishmongers believe that the mental aspects of their work are as critical to their success as the
physical aspects of their work because the mental aspects
help them to maximize every opportunity to be great.
Their work involves a lot more than throwing fish!

The following story, told by Darren, reveals some of the
mental aspects of being great. He believes part of being
great is being aware of his intention as well as of what he
says and does. He also believes that this has carried over
to his personal life. Since he has been working at World
Famous Pike Place Fish, Darren has found a much greater
awareness of his thoughts, words, emotions, and intentions,
which has truly changed the way he relates with people.

When I started working at Pike Place Fish,
I expected a normal fish market. I expected
to be cutting up fish and all of the physical
mechanics of the job. What I found was there
is much more behind the scenes that people
are not aware of. Pike Place Fish is a way of
life. Being great affects everything from the
quality of our product and the operations of
our fish market to the way I am with customers and my coworkers.

As a result of his awareness of being and doing, Darren
cannot ignore how his words affect others. It is a constant
process because the fishmongers talk to people all day.
His awareness of his thoughts and how he interacts with
other people has made Darren see that he is part of a bigger vision at Pike Place Fish. He is a contributing member
of a great team, and his contribution changes every day.

Another thing I've learned about greatness is
how to have integrity in my life. We talk about
it at our meetings, and it made me really think
about the word *integrity* and what it means to
me. Integrity means different things to different
people, but to me it means keeping my word
and being honest. Being aware and having
integrity mean being a powerful, positive,
great human being.

Darren

There is a choice involved in committing to the fishmongers' set of beliefs. The commitment to Pike Place Fish is viewed as an invitation. When a new fishmonger is hired, inviting them to learn the mental as well as physical aspects is a much more powerful approach than imposing, or forcing them to commit to, something they may not believe. At Pike Place Fish, each fishmonger is committed to being world famous, each is committed to assisting their fellow crewmembers to be the greatest they can be, and each is committed to making a positive difference in people's lives.

Each fishmonger came to Pike Place Fish to meet people, to enjoy a great work environment and, of course, to throw fish. No one knew, until work started, that they would get a whole lot more than they bargained for. The following story from Sammy offers a peek at life in the midst of transformation. As one of the managers, he believes that in order for greatness to occur, everyone has to be in it together. Even when Sammy himself began to transform, he did not notice he was changing, but he certainly noticed the change in everyone around him.

> As Pike Place Fish transformed, I didn't even notice things changing. I just noticed everyone around me changing. That's what personal and organizational transformation looks like.
>
> One thing that makes our crew great is the mental part of our work. I tell them that the mechanical operations are easy — an eight-year-old could learn it pretty quickly. The

mental part is a little more difficult. When a new hire has got the mental part understood, they come out of their shell. Eventually, they all do, but the secret is finding a way as their manager or coach to get them out of their shell faster, and in such a way as to not drive him into himself, drive him away, or make him defensive. That's my ongoing challenge here. When I'm at ease and don't have to worry, it is because the crew is really *on*.

My role is to coach them to be managers. They do the mechanical and the mental work on their own. If any of them sees something wrong, he or she isn't going to stand there or turn away without saying something. Because they feel like they each own this place, they act accordingly. Regardless of what the problem is, each will correct what they encounter, either physically in the shop or mentally within themselves and with each other.

Sammy

Path to Greatness

You may be wondering how one goes about starting the process of transforming from ordinary to great. The power of the fishmongers' transformation comes from their ability to recognize their intentions, and from the underlying realization that they create every choice in their lives.

Remember the crew's adage: It's all over here. Their reactions, their thoughts, and the outcomes they experience are theirs to own. They are all of it — the good, the bad, and the ugly.

Darren's story demonstrates his transformation at Pike Place Fish. His experiences have given him tools to make choices in his life that he previously did not know he could make. The principles of Pike Place Fish have taught him how to deal more effectively with everyday issues and challenges. His biggest realization is that he has a choice in every matter.

> Doing things differently can be a form of transformation, but what we are about at Pike Place Fish is a transformation of being. I can choose who I want to be in my life at any moment. I can choose to be happy or angry, fearful or loving.

Before Darren figured out that he always has a choice in the matter, it seemed that negative things would come up out of the blue, and he would get upset. He needed tools to deal with these unexpected events, and one tool that he got from Pike Place Fish was the ability to look at his initial reaction when something happened. He would ask himself, "What happened, and how am I going to choose to react?" He learned that he has a choice: to be upset about something or to choose to create a possibility out of what had happened.

One of the great things about Pike Place Fish
is that we have an agreement to help each
other when any of us is having a problem with
something or is upset about something. Having them listen to me, or whatever is bothering
me, helps me get back on track quickly. After I
talk about what upset me, I can move forward.
If I pretend that I'm not upset, it just takes
that much longer. Knowing I have a choice in
how I react to things has made all the difference in the world.

Darren

When you are able to see you have a choice in how you
live your life, you will find the ability to change your experience at any given moment. The fishmongers actually
choose how they will experience a situation or an event;
in effect, they choose how they want to experience their
reality. Though it is true that our perceptions determine
our reality, one might define *reality* as "who we are being
in relation to what we see, what we do, how we think, and
how we feel." No two human beings experience the same
reality, nor do they relate in the same way to what they see
or do.

What you experience in your life is a result of what you
call forth from the choices that you make. The fishmongers
have found that they can add value to their life experiences
through their thoughts and language. Language is a formal system to qualify and quantify our experiences. The
fishmongers use language to invent or change their reality.

You, also, can choose to invent or to reinvent yourself, your reality, and your life experience at any given moment.

Doug's story is a great example of how he chooses the meaning of his work. Doug's work could be described in a number of different ways, and each description would call forth a different experience for him, but he chooses to call it *fun!*

> For me, it's easy to be upset about having to get up in the morning. I have to be at the Market at 6:30, chopping ice with cut-up hands from the day before — 6:30 in the morning in Seattle, Washington! Not too many jobs begin then, and I end the day at 6:30 at night. I bust my buns the whole time. And have fun? Yep. There are people that make at least twice as much as I do, not doing as much physical and mental work as I do, and they choose to not have fun. People come down to the Market, sharing their problems at home and at work. They don't see that they have a choice to make it what it is.
>
> If people could see the choices I make and what I do at the fish market day after day — there is no way that people couldn't experience the same transformation to greatness at a barber shop, a corporate office, an accounting office, a bank, or a grocery store. It's not about throwing fish — we all know that. It's what you choose to have happen. Aside from the fun, I

have an underlying commitment, something to
hold on to, because when the fun and the throwing is gone, and when the hype is gone, then
what? When it is freezing at 6:30 in the morning, there's my choice and my commitment.

Doug

World Famous Pike Place Fish creates and chooses experiences collectively. For example, the notion of "world
famous" was created out of *not* being known by the
world. At one particular meeting, Jim was coaching the
fishmongers on creating a more inspiring future. One of
the fishmongers decided that a more inspiring future
could include becoming world famous. So, though they
were unknown by the world at that time, they added
"World Famous" to their logo and on the shipping boxes.
Because they chose to be world famous, opportunities for
recognition and fame started to present themselves.

Each fishmonger's personal transformation grew out
of a willingness to be open to something new and different
from what he or she currently knew, and this willingness
resulted in something quite amazing: The universe listened.
Things started happening, and it appeared as if Pike
Place Fish realized opportunities – appearing seemingly
out of nowhere – that otherwise may have not shown up.

The next story, told by Bear, demonstrates the meaning
of this openness to the new and different. Bear's willingness
means finding ideas that fit into his life, and being okay
with coaching or being coached by other fishmongers in a
way that leaves everyone feeling powerful.

I used to drive the truck, and there are lessons that all of the people that drive the truck to pick up fish need to learn but hesitate to, because it means that they have to come out of their shell and create a relationship with someone. If I create relationships at all of the places I go, I will get great service. If I order something from a salesperson without creating a relationship, I am going to get what everybody else gets. The relationship causes people to go that little extra step to make sure I get what I really want. They start looking out for me.

When Johnny offered Bear a job at Pike Place Fish, Bear recognized that his job included the idea that no matter what he was doing, he needed to build the same type of relationship with others that Johnny built with him. The difference between Pike Place Fish and ordinary organizations is that Bear (like the other fishmongers) chooses to take ownership and responsibility for what he is doing, rather than just doing what he is supposed to do. Instead of getting a piece of paper and filling an order on it, Bear treats the paper as if someone is standing in front of him.

The beauty is that there isn't a list of things you have to do to be like Pike Place Fish, which can be frustrating for people looking for a quick fix or recipe. It is an individual commitment, and if everyone is committed to moving the same direction, your team can do anything. That is one of the reasons that we have our meetings every other week. The meetings give us an opportunity to share our individual commitments. It's extraordinary that an employer would allow me the opportunity to participate in the business as more than just an employee.

Bear

The path to greatness is a journey. It involves many different insights and underlying beliefs. It involves a willingness to be open to something new and different, and to be responsible for one's own thoughts, words, and actions. It also involves having a purposeful intention. The last story in this chapter is told by Chris. It is powerful because it brings to light how simple these concepts are, yet how profound the collective effect can be.

"World peace is an idea whose time has come" is a powerful statement. I remember hearing Johnny say that a couple of days after I started working at Pike Place Fish. At the time, I thought, "What the hell is this guy talking about? I am here to drive a truck, throw some fish, and play. Is he out of his mind?" It took a while, but I realize it is the most sane thing I've heard.

At Pike Place Fish, I've learned that I have more power than I ever realized. Before working here I wasn't necessarily a victim, but I tended to react to what was happening in my life rather than being proactive and living the life I wanted. I know obstacles will still show up. But now I can choose what I need to do to always be in line with my intention.

At the Market, I notice people have a tendency to take themselves too seriously. Even reading this story, people may miss things if they analyze every detail, wondering what to do next. When it comes down to it, it's pretty simple: Recognize who it is that you want to be and just be that. Each person has to choose for him or herself. It's really that simple.

As a result of working at Pike Place Fish, Chris has learned to live his life more powerfully. He has realized that everything that occurs in his life relates directly to his intention. While he used to live his life as if everything that happened was happening *to* him, he now realizes whatever happens in his life was created *by* him — either knowingly or because he wasn't being aware. He has learned that when he chooses to make someone's day, he gets as much out of it as they do, if not more.

To see someone being negative isn't acceptable to me anymore. If I let them continue on, they are going to spread negativity to everyone they come into contact with. That is not in line with my commitment to a world full of possibilities and positive energy. At my fish market, I give them a reason to smile.

Imagine the possibilities in a world where people got upset, dealt with it, and grew from it. Imagine a world where people knew that they could be perfect just the way they were. Imagine a world where nations saw each other as caring societies, where other cultures were equally valued. I think it is possible, by being aware of the impact that one person has on another human being and choosing to make a positive impact.

Chris

Review of Chapter 2

✳ It's all over here.

✳ The *catch* is that ordinary happens and greatness is generated.

✳ Being ⟶ Doing ⟶ Having:
Your core beliefs and underlying assumptions (*being*) will determine your actions and behaviors (*doing*), which results in outcomes (*having*).

✳ Be great in all that you do.

✳ Nothing happens *to* you. Things happen, and you choose how to respond.

3 Intention and Commitment

Communicating through Intention

Have you ever thought about your intention in life? If you knew that a commitment to your intention would affect all of the relationships in your life, wouldn't you take some time to think about it? One of the steps on the path to greatness is to live with a conscious purpose or intention. Unless you have been living your life with a conscious purpose or intention, you have to assume that, up to this point, your experiences are the result of an unconscious intention.

The fishmongers have each developed personal as well as collective intentions and commitments. We invite you to take a moment and think about the following questions:

✴ What is your intention?

✴ Is your intention clear to all those around you?

✳ What is your commitment at work, at home, to yourself, and to others?

✳ What is it that guides you into your future?

At Pike Place Fish, the fishmongers foster a collective intention to make a positive difference in people's lives, and they are committed to one another's greatness. Their commitment allows each fishmonger the opportunity to be great and to do amazing things. When you allow the people around you to know your intention and commitment, they will be equally committed to you—possibly even more committed. Intention and commitment often go hand in hand, as Andy's story indicates.

Andy believes much of what you see at Pike Place Fish has to do with intention. He feels that being aware of his own intention means putting aside all of the other thoughts in his head. He practices it at work and in his personal life. Having an awareness of his intention and a commitment to making his intention occur has had a powerful effect on his relationships with his friends, his family, and his coworkers.

> I've taken much of what we do here at Pike
> Place Fish and started practicing it with my
> family. I've realized from my intention and
> commitment that the little things (like getting
> into arguments with my family) are really
> minuscule compared to the commitment that
> I have to loving my family and having them in

Andy and Anders

my life. I see how my intention and commitment affect relationships in my life and remind
myself, "You know what? My commitment to
them is that I love them, and they are my life.
This argument is really minuscule and not
worth wasting our time together." My intention and commitment give me perspective.

Andy

In order for a transformation from ordinary to great to
occur, the fishmongers must allow their intentions to
guide them. There is no magic formula or procedure for
achieving greatness. They simply have to start being
great in everything that they do. They have to live in a
manner that reflects greatness, and the outcome will

show up as greatness. World Famous Pike Place Fish first created a collective intention and organizational vision to become world famous, and they have now expanded their intention and vision to making a powerful and positive difference in people's lives.

Matt's story demonstrates his process of becoming aware of his intention and of how his intention guides his actions and behaviors. His intention was to work at Pike Place Fish, and following that intention he committed to making it happen.

> Since I'm the new guy here, I pick up new concepts all the time. I believe I can make the best or worst out of any situation — it's all in my attitude. I came out here last Christmas, saw these guys, and thought, "Wow! I belong here. I want to do this." I knew it was a hard job to get but I didn't care.
>
> People still ask me, "How'd you get that job?" I know it was because of my intention to get this job. Following my intention made me drive out from Pullman every other weekend to talk to the crew about working here — at six A.M. for just five minutes. Now I work here. The power of making that happen made me see I can do that with most anything in my life. As a result, I've become much more aware of my intention and my commitment in all that I do.
>
> It's interesting to watch the guys and see how their intention drives them. For example,

it might start getting a little slow at the Market, and one of us will pick up the energy and get the crowd into it by getting a customer to go behind the counter and catch a fish. Sometimes we have to remind ourselves of our intention and goals. Just like flipping a switch, we find our commitment and have fun. When the energy is good, things flow for hours out of the day. It's an unspoken agreement we have with each other to be aware of our team's intention.

Matt

Ryan reflects on how he demonstrates his intention to create relationships when taking care of customers. It is not something that he has to work at doing; it comes quite naturally out of his intention. The fun is the natural outcome of being aware of his intention and commitment.

I create a great environment for visitors to let loose and be themselves without judgment. A lot of people watch us for hours because they don't experience that in their jobs or their relationships. I've been in this environment for so long I can't imagine not having this education, if you will, on life, work, and how to relate with people. What people see is simple, but they try to make it so complex. When it comes down to it, we are all just human beings creating this crazy thing we call life [*laughing*].

Ryan believes visitors to the Market fail to see that what the fishmongers do involves so much more than just having fun. Customers think that having fun is the fishmongers' only goal, instead of getting what is behind the fun. The life lesson that Ryan learned from Pike Place Fish is that he can really do anything he wants as long as he creates the intention and makes a conscious choice, a commitment, to making it happen.

One time, I had a customer who was interested in spending one hundred dollars on salmon. I was talking and visiting with him, and he was having a great time. I listened to him share information about himself, and he just kept adding more to his order. Instead of one half of a salmon, he bought three whole salmon. Instead of two pounds of king crab, he took home a whole box and said he was going to throw them in the freezer.

My intention wasn't for him to buy more — my intention was just to have a good time, have him feel good and be excited with his experience. So later, when he pulls the seafood out of his freezer to prepare a meal, it refreshes his memory of the time that he had with me at Pike Place Fish. I want him to think, "Wow! That was a great time I had when I bought this king crab."

I am sending customers away not just with our product, but with an experience that goes along with the product. It's just amazing; it doesn't have anything to do with making the sale. In fact, when I am with someone, just really having a good time with that person, it's easy to create a relationship with them. They get the full World Famous Pike Place Fish experience.

Ryan

As Ryan's story demonstrates, when he is aware of his intention he accesses the power to realize outcomes that he may not have even considered. Just as they generate greatness, the fishmongers generate new intentions all the time. The more intentional they are in any given situation — in a relationship or in a collective group of like-minded individuals — the more successfully they are able to achieve the desired outcome.

There are many management books and business models in the world today, but if the intention does not change at the underlying, gut level, the outcome remains the same. For example, after one fishmonger suggested becoming world famous, all the others had to buy into the intention to *be* world famous. They also had to figure out what this meant to them, individually and as a group. The moment they created the intention to be world famous, each started behaving as if they were already world famous. Their actions and activities supported their intention.

The outcome of that decision was that things started happening — the universe was listening, so to speak — and new opportunities began to present themselves. The fish market has been featured on several television shows and in several magazines. Moreover, with the exception of the Pike Place Fish website, they haven't spent a dime on advertising; they just created an intention and committed to being "World Famous" Pike Place Fish, and the rest is history.

The following story demonstrates how Anders views life at the Market. He recognizes that other people may have jobs in more comfortable conditions, but he has created a system for putting his intention into practice. He believes that if he can make it happen in his working environment, you can too. Recognize how often choice plays a role in his awareness of intention and commitment.

A lot of people may go through life unhappy with their work environment, and they might think it's easy for me at the fish market because my work is inherently fun and easy. I mean, most people who are resisting changing their work environment think all we do is throw fish and holler a lot.

Here's the real deal: I've heard people say, "It can't be fun at my work because I sit in an office all day." Well, consider this... Your office is forty to fifty degrees warmer than it is at the fish market in the wintertime. I get up when it's dark and freezing outside, and I don't want to get out of bed. I choose to get out of bed, make a conscious choice to come to the Market, and have a clear intention of making a

difference in people's lives. What's here to
greet me? A bunch of ice! I have to put my bare
hands in the ice to set up our shows, and I
have to have a warm pan of water to stick my
hands in to defrost them — at 6:30 A.M. I'm here
twelve hours a day, and it's slow and rainy in
the wintertime. It's not like summertime,
when people are here from all over the world
to visit Pike Place Fish.

Anders's work environment would be considered miserable by most people, so when people tell him they can't
have fun at work, Anders has a hard time understanding
their complaints. He loves his job and the environment he
works in — even in the wintertime. He typically stays late
to do the deliveries, and when he goes home it is dark,
cold, and rainy. The driving conditions and traffic are dangerous. Yet he loves it; he's happy and fulfilled.

Many mornings, I sit on the edge of my bed
after turning off my alarm and play this game
of how I want my day to go — creating it. The
game of the day is, "What do I want to have
happen today?" If I say what I want to happen
that morning and really mean it, I don't have
to do anything out of the ordinary and I experience exactly what I want. It's crazy.
    One morning, the game was to be in a rela-
tionship with every person with whom I came
in contact. Throughout that day I was getting

many tips. People were giving me fives and
tens like it was nothing. One guy gave me a
$40 tip on a $120 sale, and it wasn't because I
said, "I am going to get a bunch of tips today."
I simply said, "I'm going to create relationships
with people today." Out of that, people wanted
to be in a relationship. It's weird how it happens. They sensed my genuine care for them.

It's the best way for me to start my day —
before I interact with anybody or anything.
Just sitting on my bed in the morning and
being conscious of how I want my day to go
creates how my day goes. It's laying the foun-
dation or the groundwork for a great day. If I
say that nothing is going to get in my way that
day, then nothing will get in my way.

Anders

What Is Your Intention?

In the following story, Russell demonstrates how being
clear about his intention to take an interest in the life of
another human being opened up a completely new possibility in his own life. He realized he could experience the
kind of life he wanted. Taking an interest in the lives of
others has had a powerful effect on his work life; now his
intention is reflected in his home life as well.

Something different than what I expected
when I started at Pike Place Fish was the

whole notion of knowing what my intention is. I realize everything occurs in my life as a result of my intention. This way of life isn't just about the fish, the throwing, or the yelling. It's the intention to create relationships with people as much as it's about selling fish and making money. We are here to make a difference. There is no separation between my work life and home life. I might be in a different place, but I'm always living it.

One of the funniest things that I've noticed at the Market is when I say "Hi" to people, they usually respond with "Just looking." I'll repeat, and say, "How are you doing?" It's funny how people are so quick to shut down. I think people rarely take an interest in the life of another human being anymore. I do that here at Pike Place Fish, and it surprises people. I often wonder what keeps people from sharing with each other — with coworkers or customers. When I started playing with that intention in my life, things began to change.

Russell

At every moment, there is choice. The fishmongers can choose to be ordinary, to do their job and to let the goals be a place to *get to*, or they can choose greatness, to be aligned in their intention and to use the goals as a place to *go from*. What do you stand for? What is it that you are passionate about? What dreams or goals keep you up at night? What inspires you to get out of bed in the morning? The fishmongers let whatever that happens to be to guide them, as individuals and collectively, at Pike Place Fish. They are very conscious of their intentions and of whether they are aligned with their commitment day after day.

When the fishmongers become conscious of their intention and allow it to guide them, the next step is to choose to live it, and this choice is made repeatedly. There is *always* choice because there are always obstacles or curveballs that make the fishmongers conscious of their intention once again.

Along with an awareness of intentions, the fishmongers also are aware of the concept of *commitment.* Most of us already know what commitment means, but to the fishmongers commitment means taking a stand for what their intention is and for what they believe. For the fishmongers, it means being world famous, making a difference — and throwing a lot of fish! Commitment is a pledge that compels the fishmongers to fulfill their intentions.

Once an intention is established and a commitment is made, the next step involves relinquishing attachment to the outcome. The fishmongers say that relinquishing attachment to the outcome means "surrendering it to the universe." This surrender creates the opportunity and the space for unexpected things to happen, though it appears as if the universe presents opportunities from nowhere.

To surrender is to relinquish an attachment to the outcome; you cannot be attached to what you do not know is going to occur. Conversely, if you are attached then you are unable to allow any other possible outcomes to occur. There may be something far better than what you dreamed possible, but you may not see it if you remain attached to your own idea of what the outcome should be. Thus, attachment to a specific outcome is dangerous because you will inevitably tie your expectations to it.

After working for even a short time at Pike Place Fish, the fishmongers' intentions and commitments start to resonate throughout their lives. This can be seen in their personal goals, in their relationships with friends and family, and in their dreams and aspirations. Jaison tells a story that demonstrates his commitment to himself and to Pike Place Fish. It represents a good example of the struggle some people contend with when trying to balance dreams and aspirations with work.

> I'm a drummer in a band, and everything I
> experience at the Market I also experience
> with my music. The concepts are the same
> but the environments are different. My band
> Severhead plays heavy rock or jazz-influenced
> music. It was a commitment I made to play
> music, and while I didn't know how it would
> happen, I knew it would.
>
> Johnny and I met for coffee, and I told him
> about my commitment to play music. I said,
> "I love working here, but if I want to be happy
> I need to modify my work schedule." He asked
> what kind of schedule I needed and I told him

which days. He made it happen. I thought, "Wow! This guy is really committed to me." It reinforced my commitment to him and made a huge impact in my life.

Honestly, I don't think enough people pursue their dreams outside of work. If I go to work and don't take care of what I want or need to maintain my health and happiness, I end up working for someone else's dream. Pike Place Fish is Johnny's dream; this is what he has put his whole life into. But I also have dreams and want them to be successful. We've recorded two CDs and we're always progressing. This wouldn't be possible without my commitment to myself and to Pike Place Fish.

Jaison

Results of Your Intention

Justin's story is about the result of being conscious of intention and commitment, about stopping for a moment and focusing within himself. Justin works to be aware of every moment and to recognize that he has the choice either to accept what life offers or to redefine it.

Every morning, when I wake up, I don't want to get up. So right then and there I say, "Who am I going to be today? Am I going to be Justin that wants to get back in bed, or am I going to actually go down to the Market, be present in

my life, and make a difference for people?"
When I don't consciously sit there and do that,
I'm choosing to not be conscious and get
whatever shows up.

When I choose to make a difference for
people, my day goes much better — it's just the
way it works for me. I'm like everyone else: I'm
a dude that wakes up in the morning to go to
work because I have bills to pay. But if I didn't
sit and become conscious of my intention
every day, work might suck.

The people who see the fun at Pike Place
Fish sometimes don't see what's behind it, and
they just want that — the fun. It takes a little
mental work and a commitment, but the outcome is worth it. I used to think you couldn't
teach an old dog new tricks. Well, start being
willing, old dog, and you will be able to roll
over [*laughing*]. I can be set in my ways too,
and I know how tough I make it for myself
sometimes.

If I had to stop throwing fish, Pike Place
Fish would still be the same place. I'd simply
invent it to be different. Pike Place Fish is not
going to stop being fun if I stopped throwing
fish because the fun doesn't come from throwing fish. It comes out of choosing my intention
every day.

Justin

You may be wondering how to start on your path to greatness in your own life. At Pike Place Fish, it begins with an individual commitment to make a collective difference in the world. It is all part of the human experience. For the fishmongers, the essence of having fun comes from what the crew does in order to support their vision of making a difference to people.

In creating your intention, therefore, recognize that the point is not so much achieving the goal of the intention or "getting there"; the point is that your intention is reflected in your lifestyle. As your awareness increases, you may begin to see how your actions and behaviors are connected to your intention. The fishmongers see their intention as a great opportunity to make a positive impact in the world.

The best part of creating an intention is that it can be as expansive as you choose. For example, if your intention involves making a difference within the boundaries of your organization, your actions and behaviors will reflect that intention. However, if you expand your intention to include making a difference not only in your work environment but also to your family and friends, your actions and behaviors will also alter to reflect this greater intention. Eventually, as your intention to make a difference expands to include your community or your nation, who you are being is further altered. Finally, if you continue to expand your intention to include not just the people of the world but also the animals, plants, and environment—all aspects of the world—your actions and behaviors will reflect your expansive intention and commitment. If humans did this collectively, we could realize global stewardship!

The last story includes a very powerful example from Jeremy, who was diagnosed with a tumor on his brain stem in March 2002. It is an amazing look at what resulted when he used his intention and commitment to deal with his diagnosis. Jeremy went back to work at Pike Place Fish full-time in October 2002, just as he said he would. How did he do it? Let's see.

Pike Place Fish has taught me how I am choosing to deal with my diagnosis. As soon as I started feeling symptoms — I had a headache and heard humming in my ears — everyone kept telling me to go to the doctor. I was worried because it was almost summer, it was going to be busy, and I didn't want to take time off work. I love summer. Never in my wildest dreams did I expect this.

I went to the doctor and he told me I had a golf ball–sized tumor in my brain. Sammy gave me the next week off to figure things out. It was the middle of March, and I worked when I could. They continued to give me opportunities to present at seminars to corporations, and I never felt shut out because of this brain tumor. I acted as if these were my days off. It's something that I had to deal with, and I knew the guys were here to deal with it with me.

At first, my doctors didn't know if they were going to have to operate or if radiation would work. I probably wouldn't have lived if they had operated, because of where it was located. It was dead center on top of my brain stem, and they couldn't even do a biopsy because the biopsy could have killed me. They said I'd have a whole month before they'd know anything. All I could think was that I didn't expect this to happen to me, but I did not want to spend the last month moping around thinking, "Oh, I'm gonna probably die." I wanted to just have fun and live a powerful life. So that's what I did. I had to be very conscious of my thoughts about it. There was nothing that I could do, so I might as well create it to be what it is.

There's an environment, a feeling, an energy at Pike Place Fish. The people I've met, the other fishmongers, and Johnny make me want to be here. I felt bad to call in sick, and hadn't been there for five months. I felt like I was letting my coworkers down because they had to hire two new people to replace me. Some people had to work longer hours because of my brain tumor.

Jeremy finished his third round of chemo, and the doctors wanted him to wait a month before they did another MRI. During that time, Jeremy could not work because his blood counts were low and changing daily, and his doctors did not want him stressed out from work. Jeremy also had to start exercising because he had experienced muscle atrophy. When he was able to come back to the Market he began by working half days to get his energy up and looked forward to being back full-time.

> Another thing I learned through all of this is the power of my thoughts. It gives me power to think, "I'm not going to get sick." When I say that, that is what happens. I used the power of my thoughts with the brain tumor from the beginning. I am going to get through this.

Everything went as planned except that after twenty-five days of radiation—when the doctors expected the tumor to be virtually gone—the tumor had only shrunk to one quarter of its original size, so Jeremy endured one more round of chemotherapy. He told himself that he would not get sick from the chemo, and he never did—he was never even nauseous. That is pretty powerful in itself.

> I've lost all my hair... but I kind of wanted to see what it would be like [laughing]. But when I look at myself when I get out of the shower, I think, "Ooh, I don't know about this." The whole thing is scary, but being able to tell myself how I am going to experience it has really worked for me. It is not just because of my cancer, but at Pike Place Fish, when you say

that you're going to do something, your team-mates know that you're committed. It's the integrity of my word that makes it possible.

It might sound strange, but there is a lot of power in just being with this whole thing. I get an hour or two of sleep at night and I'm wide awake all day. I decided to just tell myself that I'm nocturnal, an insomniac that doesn't need sleep [*laughing*].

Seriously, I am choosing to make this a powerful event in my life that I will look back at someday and be proud of how it all un-folded. Nobody in his right mind would ever expect this to happen to them, but when it does it is so important to know that all is not lost. It's just a matter of making it a powerful chapter in my life experience.

Jeremy

Review of Chapter 3

✳ Actions and behaviors are derived from your commitment to making your intended goal occur.

✳ In order for a transformation from ordinary to great to occur, you must allow your intentions to guide you.

✳ Once you establish your intention and commit to making that outcome happen, you must relinquish your attachment to the outcome, and let the possibilities unfold.

4 Opportunities and Transformation

Oh, the Possibilities!

The individuals that comprise Pike Place Fish's world famous crew stand for and inspire the greatness of one another. Collectively, the crewmembers look each day for opportunities to make a powerful and positive difference in the lives of their customers. It is possible for one person to influence the way other people experience life. Collectively, that opens the door to many possibilities to make a difference. This is their commitment.

At various moments in all of the fishmongers' careers, each has faced conflict, confrontation, an experience with an unhappy customer, or problems with a coworker. In those moments, the fishmongers have an opportunity to choose how they are going to participate in and experience the situation. The outcome is a direct result of the choices they make along the way. The good news is that at every moment there is an opportunity to change the course of the situation, and each situation is made up of hundreds or thousands of such opportunities.

In the following story, Bugge faces an unhappy customer named Sarah. There are several times during Bugge's story that could have gone many different directions. Because of his commitment to making a difference, however, Bugge chose to make this a positive and powerful experience. As you read his story, remember the fishmongers' underlying belief that "it's all over here." Watch how that belief, combined with Bugge's intention and commitment, affected the outcome of this situation.

One time a regular customer of ours placed an order and someone threw a fish over her head, getting a little ice on her. At the time, I was helping her and she said, "That is exactly the reason that I don't come to this f - - - ing place." I could feel myself getting defensive because I thought, "You're talking about *my* place." She said, "You guys do all this hollering... all you care about is the tourist. What about us, the people who live here?"

I said, "I hear what you're saying. There are a lot of people that feel the same way. But what I need to get clear to you, if at all possible, is that we create an environment that is fun, and people like to come and hang out. Whether you live here or not, we want you to feel like you had a good experience. And if you are ever uncomfortable with anything, please let me know, because I want to make sure that you're happy. I don't want anything to come between the relationship we have, although I don't even know your name..." She said, "My name is Sarah." I said, "Hi, Sarah. My name's Dan, but they call me Bugge."

The fact that Bugge recognized Sarah was right was a moment that could have gone several different directions. Bugge could have thought, "Who cares? I'm going to sell this if you buy it or not. Your five dollars isn't going to make or break this store." But that is not Bugge's commitment, and it is not aligned to the vision of Pike Place Fish. Instead, Bugge told Sarah that she is their number one priority, and that her one pound of salmon once or twice a week is more important than the onetime $300 sale. Bugge told her that if she ever came by and could not get up to the counter because of the crowds, she should walk around to the side and get his attention. He made a commitment to instantly help her. It was a moment to see what possibility could come out of this negative situation.

Close to a month went by before I saw her again, and in the meantime I didn't know if I made my point clear and thought she would shop someplace else. Then one day she came back and said, "No one had ever shown any attention to me while buying a fish like you did.

I'm sorry if I left abruptly, but I just didn't know how to react with what you told me."
It really touched me.

Sarah taught me that sometimes things need time to grow and develop, and it made me wonder if she might deal with people differently. That's where making a difference comes from. I can create an opportunity out of something negative, and that's the best feeling in the world. With my commitment, making a difference occurs the way I want it to. It's not just putting on a happy face. I am the reason that this happened the way it did.

Bugge

Bugge's intention to make a difference for others has made him more responsible for his own commitment. Each fishmonger helps every other, every day, through coaching. The fishmongers are not always one hundred percent aware, but by constantly working at it and coaching one another, they quickly catch themselves. That is what makes Pike Place Fish great!

Being open and willing is a direct line to transformation and to new opportunities. An opportunity can be viewed as a favorable junction of circumstances or as a good chance for advancement or growth. There is always a possibility to make a difference and to create joy in people's lives. Pike Place Fish is a work environment where fun and joyfulness occur naturally. In order to create such an environment, though, each fishmonger has taken personal responsibility for the fulfillment of the Pike Place Fish vision: It's all over here.

At the very moment they open themselves up to new opportunities, the right people, the right circumstances, or the right something happens. Jaison's next story illustrates this tendency: As one opportunity presented itself, more opportunities began to show up. In this particular story, Jaison talks about how his band had gone through several bass players over the course of almost a year, and they needed to find someone more permanent.

> My band needed to find a bass player. We got aligned to the characteristics we were looking for and committed to finding one for our band. We also put a date on it. When I'm creating a new opportunity for myself, I like to put a date or a deadline on my goal. When I do that, I find I share with more and more people. That results in opportunities that would have never shown up otherwise. I told my band, "Let's have a bass player by June" (at the time, June was three months down the road), and out of the blue I ran into this guy I grew up with who used to play bass. I couldn't have planned it better myself.
>
> *Jaison*

Jaison told his friend that his band was looking for a bass player, without knowing what would happen. He thought it was odd to have this experience, since he had just told the band they would have a bass player by June. The other guys didn't believe him when he said it, but it worked! Jaison's friend became Severhead's new bass player before June.

Looking for Opportunities

By being open to new opportunities, the fishmongers create opportunities they may not otherwise experience. If we are living an ordinary life, we simply accept whatever is thrown our way, and we react to it as if there is only one path. On the path to greatness, however, the fishmongers realize that there are an infinite number of paths on which to venture. You are the only limitation in your life, and being open to new opportunities makes life quite exciting because opportunities are always presenting themselves!

For example, Ryan was looking for an opportunity to play college baseball. At the time, he was in high school and working part-time at Pike Place Fish. It had been a longtime goal of his to play college ball, and after hearing so many stories from the crew, he decided to see what he could come up with in his own life.

> I wasn't the greatest baseball player, but I thought I might be good enough to play in college. After one of our meetings, I told everyone and their mother that I was going to go to college and I was going to play baseball. I was in high school at the time and didn't know if I could afford it. I didn't even know what it took

to get into college, but I knew I wanted to play ball.

I worked really hard, and during my senior year in high school I was accepted to college and recruited to play baseball. It required dedication to school and training, and the only reason I made those efforts was because of my commitment — and telling myself for about three years prior that I was going to play college ball.

When I look back to figure out how it happened, I don't really know. I just did the things, big and small, that were necessary to get myself to that point. What made me do those things was telling myself, out loud, that this was the opportunity I had been waiting for and the universe would handle the rest.

It's not like pretending and telling myself I am going to be president of the United States, when I know that it isn't going to happen because I don't want to be president (but if I wanted to be, I could!). I was inviting something new into my life, playing college baseball, that was unrecognizable to me at the time — I did not know what it was going to take to get into college and play ball. I was open to the opportunity and ready to make it happen. It's like this Zen way of living life [*laughing*].

Ryan

Creating a new opportunity, and committing to it occurring, makes all the obstacles that come up along the way tolerable because the underlying intention will be the guide through the bumps on the road. The fishmongers are conscious of their intentions and are ready for what opportunities show up. The path or several different paths will reveal themselves. On your own path to greatness, be willing to open your mind to whatever opportunities present themselves.

The fishmongers have become very effective in their lives and at work. If they don't like what they are experiencing, or if they are not open to opportunities when they present themselves, it shows up in their work, and others notice it. Some people can spend an entire career in that frame of mind and, as a result, experience a very ordinary life.

In order to create new opportunities, you must know the power of your mind. The fishmongers choose to create opportunities for themselves. They recognize they are their own greatest advocate or limitation. As Ryan said, he did not know how he would make the opportunity to play college baseball happen. He was just open to the opportunity of playing college ball and was able to seize the moment when it presented itself.

The crew is deeply committed to creating opportunities and to having a powerful purpose that gives meaning to their work. Of course, having the right attitude and the ability to see opportunities must coincide with doing the work required. There has to be a balance — intention and willingness must be balanced with productivity. The bottom line is still the bottom line. At Pike Place Fish, the bottom line is measured in flying fish.

The following story, told by Justin, demonstrates what being open to new opportunities looks like. After working at Pike Place Fish for nearly thirteen years, he has seen how many newcomers come to Pike Place Fish looking for an ordinary job and, instead, end up with a more powerful way to live their lives. He recognizes the difference between new fishmongers who are open to something new and those who are not. He has also realized in his work that people (coworkers and visitors) want to be in a place where they are supported — where they have a choice in the kind of lives they are able to live.

> When new fishmongers start their first day of work, they have no idea what they're getting into. They see the glamour but are quickly in for quite a shock. It's just that it's different enough, they will resist if they're not open to something they are not expecting. Most will be open to whatever opportunities come into the picture.

Newcomers want the freedom to be themselves, and they want to be successful at what they are learning at Pike Place Fish. That is what Justin wants, as well — to be happy at work, rather than Employee Number 428 or so-and-so from the accounting department. Pike Place Fish is all about choice; each fishmonger has a choice in every matter at every moment, and even if he or she does not choose, that, too, is a choice. Justin feels that most people do not realize that life could be different from the way that it is, and that many great opportunities pass by because people get caught up in how and why things happen and stop seeing what is right in front of them.

> For example, this morning at seven A.M. there was a tour bus passing by the fish market really slowly, and I decided to run out there along the side of the bus and throw a salmon up in the air by the windows [*laughing*]. I thought they'd think it was cool. That's one way I can create an opportunity in the moment, from what is right in front of me and what could be. Throwing the salmon up in the air was the opportunity I saw at that moment.
>
> When people ask what we do for fun, I tell them to be aware of opportunities in the moment. If I wasn't aware, I wouldn't have even seen the bus driving by, let alone the opportunity to make those people smile. I would have missed it. It's a slippery slope when you're not paying attention to where you are and what opportunity might be on its way. What I experience at Pike Place Fish is possible in any company, with any type of culture or structure, because it's a way of life, not a template to follow. It's so important for people to see the opportunities right in front of them.
>
> *Justin*

Anders makes an expert fish toss.

Because the fishmongers remain open to new opportunities, doors have opened that they never even imagined. Always being aware of an opportunity has allowed the world to open up for Pike Place Fish. Things have fallen into place in a way the fishmongers sometimes cannot explain. Instead of spending time trying to figure out how or why things happen, though, the fishmongers have learned to appreciate *whatever* is happening.

Invitation to New Opportunities

The fishmongers go about their daily business looking for opportunities to demonstrate their intention to make a difference and to demonstrate their commitment to one another. In looking for such opportunities, they have had to develop a great appreciation for a future that is un-known. Because they recognize that every moment is new, the fishmongers see themselves both walking into their futures and simultaneously disengaging from their pasts. This does not mean forgetting your past; there is a tremendous value in the experiences you have had in the past. Rather, walking into your future and disengaging from your past simply means being very, very aware of the present.

The point is that it is not the past but the opportunities that await you that determines who you are now. Each fishmonger makes World Famous Pike Place Fish exist through an awareness of the opportunities to demonstrate their individual and collective intention. They are continuously faced with new opportunities that did not exist one moment ago, and their measure of greatness comes from their potential to make a difference through such opportunities. If they choose to be unaware, they inadvertently limit the boundless opportunities that are trying to show up in their lives. They can choose to see those opportunities, and to do so at every moment... now... now... and now.

You might be thinking that this all sounds grand but that life happens, and sometimes things you didn't want show up anyway. True. However, in those moments when you are faced with something you did not expect or want, even then you have choices. You may not have a choice in whether or not the event or situation occurs; you do have a choice to be inspired by the event and to let it impel you to a greater and more powerful way of being. You can either proactively seek the new opportunities inherent in the event or you can choose to be frustrated, angry, resentful, or hurt — and let the event or the emotion take your power away.

Even if the fishmongers find themselves in a place that is not empowering, all is not lost. At that moment, they choose something different. They ask what their intention is. They could write the negative situation off as fate controlling their destiny, including their accomplishments and their failures. Accomplishment is what they bring forth from their thoughts, language, choices, and actions. When they are open to opportunities, it literally takes them to a different realm. Imagine the possibilities that await you.

The last story is Doug's. He worked full-time at Pike Place Fish to get through college and graduate school, and simultaneously grew a family of five children. When his schedule allows, he still works part-time at Pike Place Fish, and he teaches full-time at a high school. Doug realized that, by being able to see opportunities, he has learned to take responsibility for his actions and for whatever situation he may be experiencing. No matter how big the obstacle, Doug's openness to opportunities has led to a powerful way to live his life.

Because his wife has multiple sclerosis, Doug's family spends a lot of time in the doctor's office. His intention is to lighten the atmosphere, even though MS is a disease with no known cure. The ability to have fun, whenever and wherever, is the new opportunity that Doug is practicing while coping with MS.

I have come to know that nothing can be that hard. We have a serious illness in our family. My wife has MS, and my job is to make our doctors appointments fun. No one wants to go to the doctor or go through treatments, so my job is to make that fun for my wife and kids. I believe MS is going to be a breakthrough for our family — an opportunity for my kids to see what caring for other people is about.

To be able to do that, my intention is that I want my wife to be enjoying her every moment. With MS, it's very hard for her to enjoy where she is because she gets dizzy. So I'm making sure my family is healthy, and with health comes happiness. When you see us together as a family, you see happiness. I mean, we're no different than any other family. We still brush our teeth at night, go to bed on time, drink milk, and eat our vegetables, but we have fun with it.

At Pike Place Fish, it's easy. Opportunities are everywhere. I believe anything is as serious as you make it, and my wife says I make her happy. She doesn't always share my views, but she feeds off my attitude. We have little jokes, like "What? I'm late to dinner? Well, I have MS." Or if we turn in a bill late: "Hey, my wife has MS, what are you talking about?" She laughs, so it's like we can do everything wrong and it's okay. We just have to make it okay to laugh.

Doug's family has learned to be open to all new opportunities that present themselves. For example, Doug has always utilized Western medicine, but now he has opened up to the possibility that Eastern medicine could be a great opportunity. Doug's wife is doing acupuncture with some positive results.

> This is new for us. It's a curveball we were never
> expecting. Who would? It may sound crazy,
> but when you or someone in your family has
> MS, you have to make it fun. You can have fun
> with a disease. We're eating better and we are
> having fun cooking new and different foods.
> I've learned that I create what this experience
> is going to mean to my whole family now —
> and what it'll mean twenty years from now.
> We didn't choose this in our lives. Now that
> it is here, we can choose to have horrible memories from it, or we can make it an opportunity
> to be a major breakthrough in our lives and
> have wonderful memories to look back on. It's
> more fun to choose wonderful.

> *Doug*

New opportunities can be created at any and every level. On a much grander scale, the United States saw a huge opportunity when President John F. Kennedy pledged to put a man on the moon by the end of the 1960s. Landing a spacecraft on the surface of the moon could not have been realized from the systems for propulsion, navigation, and life-support that existed at the time of his 1961 declaration. No one knew how this opportunity would unfold or what new technologies would result from the original intention to put a man on the moon; however, Kennedy's declaration led to a series of creative opportunities that otherwise may not have occurred. New developments in materials, technology, and the sciences resulted from the collective activities undertaken to support this grand opportunity.

Intention resides in the context of the future, and the future is creating itself all the time, in many different ways. The fishmongers alter and transform their futures at every moment, and every moment gives them a choice to create all kinds of opportunities. Only you can consciously affect the course of your life. With each exchange with another individual or with a situation, a new opportunity can be created.

Review of Chapter 4

✳ An opportunity is a favorable junction
of circumstances, or a good chance for
advancement or growth.

✳ Every moment includes an opportunity
to change the course of a situation, and
each situation includes hundreds or
thousands of such opportunities.

✳ In an ordinary life, we simply accept
whatever is thrown our way, and we
react as if there is only one path. On the
path to greatness, however, you must
recognize that there are an infinite
number of paths on which to venture.

✳ The past does not determine who you
are now... the opportunities that await
you do.

5 | Shaping Your Reality

New Thoughts about Thinking

The fishmongers' thoughts, words, and actions reflect the way they see the world and their reality. Language is the mechanism that the fishmongers use to connect them to their customers and to one another. Language is generally considered just a tool to communicate with others, but in a more powerful way, language connects you to your reality through your thought processes.

"Thinking" is how we talk to ourselves. The function of your mind is to process bits of information into other bits. It is like an internal feedback system, and things such as self-confidence, motivation, self-esteem, attitude, and achievement are internally based and are within each person's own control. How you connect to your internal feedback system is through your thinking.

Pike Place Fish is no different from any other place when it comes to the concept of thinking. What is different is the awareness of thinking that goes along with the normal operations and physical aspects of their work. The fishmongers have realized that their personal thoughts and opinions shape the way they respond to everything in life; it also shapes how they see other people and how they think others see them. Thoughts and language shape how people view change and all of the opportunities and adversities that come with change.

The fishmongers' awareness of language has opened their minds to opportunities to transform themselves from ordinary to great. The following story from Anders demonstrates the power of changing his thinking in order to change his experience at work. When Anders started at Pike Place Fish, being with people made him feel uncomfortable and vulnerable. What he realized, however, was that this feeling was literally all in his head. When he discovered he could change his thoughts, his experience changed as well. The realization of the power of his language and his thoughts has helped Anders deal more effectively with problems. Being able to change his thinking resulted from taking responsibility for his thoughts and language.

> All the vulnerable feelings I used to have — I
> was making them up in my head. For example,
> when I was working up top, in my mind I would
> think that the people watching us were thinking
> of me in a negative way. I felt scared of failing.
> All that was really happening was people were
> standing in front of the fish market, hanging

out. The rest was just my own thoughts I made up to protect myself, and my fears.

How that changed was that I realized I could change my thoughts at any given moment. Whatever I am thinking in the moment is what's going to show up. If I'm feeling nervous and vulnerable, that's how people are going to be around me. Now when I'm out at the Market, it's just me *being* in front of a bunch of people, without my disempowering thoughts.

It has totally changed my life, because public speaking used to be my biggest fear. Even giving a speech in college was difficult. Now I do presentations in front of thousands of people and I'm comfortable. That is what *being* means to me: It's your vibe and the thoughts in your head. When you're adding all this other stuff, you create that environment. If you are comfortable with yourself, then people will see that, too. It gives them permission to be the same. That's what people see in us at the Market and what draws them here. Because of the way we are aligned and committed to making a difference, we create a lot of positive energy in our work environment.

Before working at the Market, Anders had read several books that outlined similar ideas, but Pike Place Fish has taught him how to live it. Anders learned about *willingness* from different spiritual reading and from various personal experiences. He knows that being willing is the way to allow transformation to occur, and he does not shut out anyone else's thinking just because it is different than his. He has learned to listen with an open mind. The ideas and thoughts that make sense to Anders stick with him, and over time, all those thoughts become "Anders."

Anders packages crab

Becoming more aware of my thinking has also helped me deal with problems. I had this thought: "I just want to sell fish and talk to people. I'm sick of all of these people staring at me waiting for me to do something." That night we had a great meeting and I was able to share my thoughts. From sharing that with the rest of the crew, my entire experience changed and I started having fun again.

I can be so conscious of what is going on in my head and still have these negative thoughts that keep me down at times. I think really mastering an awareness of my thinking would mean not letting my own thoughts derail me. It's human nature to sometimes have negative thoughts, but the trick is to turn down the volume or change to a more powerful station as soon as possible.

Even just everyday language and conversations bring power or take power from my life. For example, when we got stuck in traffic yesterday on the way to the airport, I realized that it was something that would have upset me in the past. I don't get frustrated when I get stuck in traffic anymore. I have learned to not resist where I am because that is where I am. The traffic is not going to go away because I'm upset. I am just going to waste that part of my life being upset, and it's not worth it to give my power away to the traffic. Things like that are insignificant in my life now.

Anders

Each of us is constantly thinking — consciously while we are awake, and through our dreams while we are sleeping. People can manage their thinking in a variety of ways, but the fishmongers have realized they have the power to change their thoughts completely. In order to know how to change their thoughts, however, they first needed to know what their thoughts were. Once they recognized their thoughts about different things, transformation became a real possibility.

At times, though, the fishmongers become very attached to their way of thinking, what they call "getting hooked" (like a fish on the line), and they may actually try to get other people to buy into their thinking as well. They may find that they catch themselves looking for ways to prove or justify their thoughts. In order to transform themselves from ordinary to great, the fishmongers have to recognize and change their thinking quickly.

If you have not really thought about thinking before, try it; once you become aware of it, life is never the same! You cannot fail to hear your thoughts once you recognize the power of your thinking, the language that you use, and how your thinking drives your actions and experiences.

As the fishmongers have become more conscious of their own thinking, they have also begun to recognize how other people think, since humans connect to others' thinking through language. When they recognize other people sharing negative thoughts about life, the fishmongers see an opportunity to bring it to light and to offer a new, more powerful thought. This concept is seen in an example given by Russell.

> At the American Society for Training and Development conference in 2001, I was there to represent Pike Place Fish. During the day, an older gentleman and his wife walked up and he asked, "Who are you?" I told him I was from Pike Place Fish, a fish market in Seattle, and told him what we do and how people have these great breakthroughs in their life. He said that it sounded like it would be good for his son-in-law, whom he did not like. I asked him

to tell me a little bit about this son-in-law. After working at Pike Place Fish and knowing "it's all over here," I have become really clear when I hear the "over there" in someone else's thinking.

The gentleman didn't think his son-in-law treated his daughter well, and he wasn't her dream man. After he finished, I told him his thoughts were actually creating the reality for the son-in-law to live into. I asked him if he would be willing to give up the kind of thinking he had about his son-in-law, for his daughter. I also told him that he needed to trust in his daughter, that she is with the man with whom she wants to be. We spoke about what it would look like if his son-in-law was really great.

All of a sudden, he changed right before me. He totally got it! I don't know what the exact trigger was, but I know it when I see it. When I saw it, I told him to call his son-in-law when he got home, and he said he would. He thanked me so much because he already had a different relationship with his son-in-law before he even left our booth. It was a powerful experience for him and his wife, and even more so for me.

There is a difference between knowing the path and walking the path. I have explored the possibility of only being limited by my thoughts. Looking at what we have accomplished, and

how the story of worldly limitations seems
to be challenged, my fish market is changing
the world.

Russell

The crew has come up with some very creative words
and ways to make a fishmonger aware of his or her thinking. Raising their own awareness has allowed the crewmembers to easily recognize when someone is being negative. If a fishmonger is hooked on negative thinking, the
crew has many ways to make him or her aware of it. You
may hear one of them make the *zzzzzz* sound — with the
image of a fishmonger leaning back pretending to be reel-
ing in a big fish with an invisible fishing pole. A finger
mimicking a hook pulling on the inside of the cheek
works equally well!

To change the language you use is, in effect, to change
your mind. Bugge tells a story about how his thinking
affected the relationships in his life. Before he worked at
Pike Place Fish, he used to think that the world was against
him. What he learned was that his need to always be
"right" kept him from having more positive and powerful
experiences. As he became more aware of the language
and thought processes he was using, he started to recognize he could have a much better experience with other
people.

I used to think I'd never get a break. I wouldn't
be able to get tickets to a show, and I'd say to

myself, "There it is again; it's because of me."
I lived via the circumstances of life, and life
created who I was, instead of me creating life.
I wasn't always thinking about it, but I won-
dered how I could get ahead with as little ef-
fort as possible.

That was me: I was a victim of life; things
just happened to me. I was defensive and tem-
peramental, always waiting for bad things to
happen to me. I didn't know it was even a possibility to go out and create something different.

When I started at Pike Place Fish, I was
resistant to any new ways of thinking — believe
it or not. I'd listen to people tell me how to do
things and nod my head and say, "Yeah, yeah,
yeah. Got it." Under my breath, I'd be saying,
"I'll make it easy on us by agreeing with you,
but as soon as I turn around I'm doing it my
way." I was resistant to coaching, listening,
and seeing opportunities for the longest time.
I thought I was really negative. I don't know if
other people could see it, but I was always in
that mode. Can you believe it? What kept me
here was the people: I loved the people I
worked with, and I loved how people perceived
us. It was instant world fame. I was this incredible fishmonger extraordinaire [*laughing*].

Then I went to this one meeting with Justin
and told him, "I hate these meetings. It's a

waste of my time. I'd rather be somewhere else." Justin said, "Try to apply it to something we do at work." I said, "I don't want to. I have fun at work." Then he said, "Then try to apply it to something in your personal life." So, I thought about the whole year and a half I'd been there. I didn't want to find anything to apply because I didn't want anyone else to be right or me to be wrong.

I decided to try to find one thing to apply, and it had to do with listening... about how I listen to others. Looking back, it was huge for my first step, and I battled with it for a long time because I always thought I was listening. I would have thousands of different responses in my head while you were speaking. I'd think, "What can I say in rebuttal?" I had to keep thinking, "Don't forget, don't forget, don't forget," what I was going to say in response. My wheels were spinning, and even if they weren't done speaking I'd jump in and say, "This is the way that it is, and that's not true."

I've realized that I'm responsible for how I listen and what my thoughts are while I'm listening. Now I can listen to you and hear what you are saying, and I don't have to interject my own thoughts. I have learned to say "I don't know" when I don't know, and to not make up thoughts about what everyone else is thinking. Now, I turn off my mind while someone is talking to me. As a result, I get more than ever out of a conversation.

Bugge

What You Say Is What You Get

The fishmongers have learned how language reflects their experience of a situation. When they are handed a situation that they do not necessarily want, they have learned that they can change their experience of the situation by changing their language and their thinking about it. The story told by Doug demonstrates how, when several circumstances occurred in his life, he was able to give the experiences the meaning he wanted. It is a wonderful example of greatness!

When I started working at the Market, I was eighteen years old and had just started college. I had fifteen credits to my name because I had gotten sick, was in a car accident, and my girlfriend was pregnant. Saying "girlfriend" now sounds weird because we've been married for eight years.

I went back to school and continued to raise my family on my Pike Place Fish income. I completed my associate's degree, and my bachelor's degree in mathematics, with a minor in Spanish. During that time, my wife and I had two more children. So by the time I was done with my bachelor's, I had three girls! (The guys would tease me: "Doug can't produce a boy"). Yeah, so that was fun [*laughing*]. So I had to go out and make a boy.

One year later, Doug completed his master's degree in education, earned his teaching certificate, started coaching basketball at Kennedy High School (south of Seattle), and continued to raise his family on his Pike Place Fish salary. Now he has finished his schooling, he owns a home, and he and his wife have added two boys to the collection.

Through this whole process, I gave meaning to all my situations. A lot of people would project their own thoughts by telling me, "You can't go back to school. You need to work, pay the bills, and raise your family." I thought I could do both — pay the bills and go to school — because I knew what I wanted to do.

For extra money, I delivered orders to the local hotels after work, for five years. When the car was full of boxes of fish, my wife and kids would walk around the Market. It was just a matter of making it fun. I didn't let the meaning of the rest of the "normal" world get to me.

To me, it's all played out right. I decided that the meaning of my experience would be whatever I wanted it to be, and I always wanted it to be positive — to be marching forward in my life. Even when it doesn't feel perfect, I always have the chance to make it perfect. Pike Place Fish is not a way of just working at the office. I want to have a great quality of life, no matter what I'm doing.

Doug

An awareness of language and thinking plays a very important role in making Pike Place Fish what it is. The fishmongers use language to call forth what they choose to experience. They incorporate personal responsibility for their thoughts, words, and actions into their daily experience through a very conscious awareness of the language they use. As Dave tells his story, you will see that he, too, has created what he wants to experience — just because he said so.

> Last semester I was diagnosed with the *E. coli* virus. The doctors told me I was really sick and said I was bound to be in the hospital for a year and wouldn't be able to graduate college on time. They said I wouldn't be able to do much of anything for one year, I would likely never be the same, and I may not be able to walk very much. But the ideas at Pike Place Fish — of not buying into what other people are saying but buying into what I'm thinking, choosing how I want to see it go, and making that happen — was really powerful for me. Given what I had learned here, I decided to think differently about it and create a better outcome to my illness.

Having *E. coli* was really intense, and knowing that words have power — what you say to yourself is what you experience — is how it really happens. If you believe in it and put value into what you say, it happens. So I put the Pike Place Fish way of being into action and I was out of the hospital after only one month. I decided I needed to graduate in June and needed to be at the Market, and when I thought about what my doctors had said, I thought, "Don't you tell me what I'm going to do and not do. Who are you to create my life?"

I thought it was odd that I got sick in the first place, and it was even more odd to hear what the doctors had said. It made me wonder where doctors are coming from when they give people a diagnosis, and why people don't know they have the power to change it. It was really a powerful experience for me, to change my fate by changing the course of what I wanted to have happen. It made me realize I can do that with lots of things in life.

At Pike Place Fish, you learn that you create your reality all the time without really knowing it. When you become aware of it, it's really powerful. With school, work, everything in my life, I can make it a good experience or a bad experience. It's more exciting to choose good.

Dave

When the fishmongers began to change their thinking about something, they noticed that the conversation with others appeared to change as well. It is not possible to tell whether their conversation really changed or if they were just finally hearing what was always being said; either way, however, the outcome is that the fishmongers have realized their inherent power to create something new — new opportunities and new possibilities. Bison describes his own experience:

> When I came back to Pike Place Fish [after working elsewhere for a while], I thought people were thinking of the old me. I thought that they were waiting for (or even expecting) me to mess up. It was just me, making it all up. I would have Bear throw me a salmon and [I'd] think, "Oh man, he thinks I'm gonna drop it." I talked to Anders about it one day and he said, "You know what? Maybe it's just you creating it. It's over here, not over there." After that, I really thought more consciously about my thoughts being over here, not over there. Then I got acknowledged for changing people's opinions of me. That was huge.
>
> There was so much wrapped up in my thoughts. I felt like everything was on my shoulders, and I had a hard time getting across some of my thoughts. It is so empowering to know that I can change that and I don't have to carry that with me. It makes me feel good to

know that I'm not the old me, and the others don't see me as the old me either. The bottom line is that if you don't enjoy who you are and what you are doing at work or at home, you should probably change your thoughts about it.

Becoming aware of your thoughts actually changes who you are. Bison's transformation was the result of realizing his need to take responsibility for his thinking ("It's all over here"). In Bison's story, you may have noticed he mentions the term *acknowledgments*. This is a reference to a segment at the end of each biweekly meeting when each fishmonger has an opportunity to acknowledge (or recognize) another crewmember for something he or she has done, and each has an opportunity to be acknowledged once by another crewmember. A fishmonger might be acknowledged for being a great listener, for giving or receiving coaching, for being fun to work with — anything that someone recognized. It is a very powerful way to end the meetings, and it is very apparent in the energy level at work the following day.

Acknowledgments have made a big difference in my life. I'll listen to someone acknowledge someone else and think, "Maybe I should start doing that." I take them as kind of a personal challenge. Acknowledgments have also helped me with my coaching. I used to be more of a "teller" — I'd say, "Do this." Now I'll ask, or show how to do something, and my intention with coaching is much clearer. I now coach in a way that includes how it is going to make us better collectively. For example, when I tell Matt that we've got to get the buckets done by 5:30 and I don't explain different ways that could help him be faster, then I'm not helping him. Powerful thinking and being acknowledged just makes me work that much harder.

Bison

Additional Thoughts about Language

The last three stories in this chapter demonstrate how your reality is shaped by your thoughts and by the language you use to communicate with yourself and others. Be conscious that your thoughts and your language also affect others. As your awareness increases, you may begin to experience more freedom to change your thinking and a greater ability to listen to others. Changing your thinking changes your experience, and you have the choice to do so at any given moment.

If I am not happy where I am, I have a choice to leave. Everything is a choice. The more times that I experience changing my thinking and seeing a different outcome, the easier it is to catch myself and change it more quickly. Once I started recognizing how I think about things, I really understood what it meant to listen, to truly hear everything that someone says to you. That was it. I recognized that there are no other thoughts in the back of my head if I am truly listening to another human being. It's really quite powerful.

Having an open mind is the most important part of thinking and listening. Not a lot of people have an open mind. People live inside their box and they want you to lead them to everything. I did, too, but then I started recognizing that, "Wow! I can lead myself!" Now, it's a matter of getting other people to that point, getting people to realize how they think about things and the language they use to communicate with others.

Andy

Your thoughts and your language may give you choices in life that you did not previously notice. Right now is a perfect opportunity to start choosing a life you want to live, rather than living a life that someone else wants you to live. Once you realize that fact, nothing can stop you except your own mind. Erik gives a great analogy for the ongoing choices in his language and his thoughts, describing it as two dogs inside his head.

The choice to be joyful isn't always an easy one. Things happen in life, and sometimes it has to be a very deliberate choice to find the positive. What I see is that I have all of these thoughts constantly running in my head. I am the one that puts the thoughts in my head, and if I choose to dwell on the negative thoughts, then that is what I get to experience: the negative. It's up to me.

The best way I can put it is what was told to me one time, and it goes like this: There are these two dogs inside of my head — one represents my positive thoughts, and the other represents my negative thoughts. They are always fighting in my head, and the one that wins is the one that I feed the most.

With one smile, I can stop and realize that life is not bad. The way I change my thinking if I'm upset is by asking myself what I am mad about. I realize it was just my thoughts. I can choose to let my thoughts affect everything I do or I can switch it in one second and say that my life is a good life. Why wouldn't I choose to be happy? Why choose to be upset or mad, and why choose to say that I hate going to work because that guy is there, or I hate that project? What I have learned is that nobody can make you mad. You make yourself mad — and you can make yourself happy, too.

Erik

Jaison gives an excellent example of this phenomenon, talking about how different types of thinking were going to either make or break a benefit concert given for one of the former fishmongers, Yori, who was injured in an accident.

It's amazing what unfolds and what you can do when you have an awareness of your thinking. It was never as apparent as this one time when my band Severhead and Michael's band World Seven decided to throw a benefit concert for Yori. After Yori's accident, we wanted to raise some money and have a great time, to celebrate Yori. It was one of those times we wanted to bring everybody together. I was sold on the idea right away, but we'd never played at a big club before. We tossed around the idea of playing at the Show Box; it's one of the best venues in Seattle. All kinds of big-name bands have played there.

So I'm thinking that it's done — I learned that from Johnny. I love thinking that way because I don't worry about all the crap that shows up along the way. When it does — because it always does — I can barrel through it and get what I want accomplished. My intention overrides any distractions or obstacles that show up along the way.

I told the guys that we were going to do a benefit concert for Yori and said, "It's at the Show Box." They said, "The Show Box? No way!" One guy said, "That'd be fun," and another guy said, "No. No way. We're not ready to play at the Show Box. No way." We only had one month to put it together.

All these things started happening as a

result of how each person was thinking about the concert. We got our first batch of two hundred tickets and they were selling, slowly. Even my mom was helping. Then someone said, "Maybe twenty dollars is too much to ask; maybe they should be ten dollars." I said, "No, this is for a benefit. It's not like this is for us. The money is going to help Yori."

All these thoughts started coming up because once you commit to something, all kinds of ideas bombard you. These negative thoughts were just killing it. I wasn't sure that it would happen. So I told the guys, "You are not going to let this thing happen with your negative thinking. You're putting all the pressure on us, and it isn't even about us. It's about Yori, and he needs our support."

After that, the band was really committed to just having fun and being in this environment of helping somebody, rather than making it our show. From changing our thoughts about it, it didn't become our show anymore, and we were a part of this big thing — bigger than all of us.

Everybody came alive. The guitar player who was so resistant in the beginning sold more tickets than anybody. The show was amazing! The whole thing turned out great. I don't think it would have happened if we had not changed our thoughts. We would have sabotaged the whole thing. That was a good lesson. After we did it, I thought, "Whoa! We just played the Show Box." It was a great opportunity for me to really experience how thinking affects life.

Jaison

Review of Chapter 5

✳ Your language and your actions reflect your thinking.

✳ Language is a powerful tool connecting you to your reality and to another human being.

✳ Changing your thinking about something will change your experience as well.

6 Problems Are a Good Thing

Communicating Problems

At Pike Place Fish, the fishmongers view problems, conflict, or differences as a good thing. Creative conflict and problems are an opportunity for learning, growth, and transformation. It would be foolish to think that conflict does not occur at Pike Place Fish — it comes up every day, just as it occurs in every other company. The difference is the fishmongers' commitment.

Each fishmonger at Pike Place Fish is committed to every other fishmonger's greatness. Imagine how it would look if you knew the people in your life were committed to your success. How would things be different from how they are now? On the other hand, if all the people in your life knew that you were committed to their success, would anything change?

Problems force the fishmongers to deal with things out in the open, when they occur. The process allows them to solve a problem or to effectively deal with a situation. Coaching is one method the fishmongers use to communicate and solve problems. Their commitment to one another's greatness alters the language they use and the tone of their voice when coaching, as well as the methods they use to convey information. Through coaching and problem-solving opportunities, the fishmongers recognize that they are each a part of something bigger, collectively, than each person is individually. These opportunities help the fishmongers stay on track toward accomplishing both personal goals and the collective goals of Pike Place Fish, as seen in Anders's story.

> Solving problems and coaching is an expression
> of my commitment, and I have to communicate
> and allow myself to be coached. That's what
> we do here. Everything's got to be out in the
> open. You can't sit there and let something
> stew — it takes away all of your power. If you
> don't communicate, there is no power in the
> relationship. If your friend or coworker goes
> somewhere else to get what they should have
> gotten in a relationship with you, then you are
> not being who you are supposed to be. You're
> not *being* your commitment to having a great
> relationship. It's never over there; it's always all
> over here. So if something's on your mind, let
> it out — now!
>
> *Anders*

When transforming a problem into an opportunity, the first step is to voice what is wrong. The fishmongers have to communicate what the problem is before they can find the opportunity in it for growth. In addition to voicing the problem, listening is a critical part of solving problems and of the coaching process. To the fishmongers, *listening* means actually hearing what another person is saying, without preparing a defense or a response during the process. The fishmonger receiving coaching actually turns off his or her thinking and allows the coach to be all that is heard.

Really listening, without having thoughts running through their heads, is what allows the fishmongers to be mentally present when assisting customers, when communicating with others, and during the coaching processes. When they listen, their own thoughts stop. The person speaking becomes the only thing heard. Being engaged in a conversation with people, and really listening to what is being said, creates relationships — the fishmongers have become experts at forming connections with other human beings. In the following story, told by Justin, recognize his attitude about problems, how he communicates problems, and how he takes responsibility for what happens.

> The majority of what bothers me in life is my
> commitment to my word and not meeting that
> commitment. For example, if I get stuck in
> traffic and am going to be late for work, I am
> not upset at the fact that I'm stuck in traffic.

I'm upset because I am committed to being at work on time, and I am going to be late. My expectation and my commitment to being on time doesn't occur. It's one of the most important things I've learned at Pike Place Fish: really realizing what specifically upsets me. It's not things out there that make me mad — it's within myself.

One day, Bugge and I had a miscommunication. It was near the end of the day, and after we were done with work I walked up to him and asked if I could talk to him for a minute. He agreed, and I told him that I thought we had a miscommunication earlier. I told him that I thought he had misinterpreted something as me not respecting him. I thought I was just saying what everybody else was saying, but I think it just sounded different to him. So I told him that the truth was that I totally respected him, that he is a great friend, and I don't disrespect friends. The whole thing was over and things were cool after that. It's never over there. It's never someone else's fault. It's always over here. If people could get that concept from the book... It is the one thing I'd want them to get.

Justin

Creative conflict in the form of debate or discussion can provide the fishmongers with opportunities to prevent the cause of the problem from showing up again. Instead of simply fixing the problem, they take it a step further and use it as an opportunity to be proactive. To get breakthrough results, generally, they have to almost invite the issue or conflict first.

Problems or conflicts most commonly occur when one of the fishmongers becomes hooked on his or her mindset. You can see it on the person's face, you can hear it in the tone of his or her voice, and the language used reflects the moment when someone is in the process of being upset. When someone is really upset, they are completely transparent, and this presents a perfect opportunity for growth and transformation. Amazingly, however, we often see another person get angry and just continue doing what we were doing — almost pretending that the person is not upset. Whether or not it has something to do with us, it still presents an opportunity to create a positive result.

To the fishmongers, problems and conflicts usually are a result of thinking, "It's all over there — it is not me." Conflict also occurs when someone does not take responsibility for what is happening. Blaming others causes problems. Dicky tells a story about a time he accepted responsibility for his thinking, and how this skill has changed the relationships in his life.

> I create my relationships to be what they are. If I have a problem with somebody else in my organization or in my family, I have to listen to what I am saying. I have to listen to my thoughts about that person. Once all of the different

thoughts I have about this person are out in the open — and when you have two people telling each other about their thoughts about each other — only then can you get a breakthrough, only then can a relationship have a new opportunity.

I know that it sounds like telling each other what is on your mind would only make things worse, but the truth is that getting my thoughts about someone out of my head allows me the opportunity to change my mind. When I change my thoughts about that person, I change my relationship with that person.

If someone still upsets me after I've changed my thoughts about him or her, I am still buying into all the circumstances and thoughts I had before. To me, that's one of the major keys: to take responsibility for my thoughts. If I am committed to a relationship with someone, then I have to also commit to being responsible for my thoughts about that person. Otherwise, we would go through a lot of people here — and we do at times — because it's hard for people to accept responsibility for their thinking. Sometimes they don't accept it until they leave; some leave because they have transformed and want to go on to pursue bigger and greater things.

Dicky

At Pike Place Fish — or anywhere — one cannot stand still, either mentally or physically. As a manager at Pike Place Fish, Dicky feels that the main thing he can offer to managers of other organizations is the ability to recognize and to change negative thinking. Taking responsibility for what shows up in his life is the path to greatness. For the principle to work in an organization, though, it has to come from the top. If top management is not generating it, then it can never trickle down to all of the other people in the organization. Moreover, each person in the organization is responsible for coaching the management's understanding.

Though coaching is a very effective way to transform problems into growth opportunities, the fishmongers do not always have the luxury of someone nearby to see them through the process. In that situation, they need to remember what their intention is. They ask themselves if who they are currently being reflects their intention and their commitment. The instant they become aware of their intention is the instant they transform their thinking. At that moment, a new opportunity is possible.

Many problems are resolved at the meetings because that is a safe environment to openly deal with conflict and problems. Everyone at the meeting, even those not directly involved, benefits from the experience. Observing someone hooked and reeled in, watching them being coached through the process, and then seeing them get off the hook is as beneficial to those not directly involved as it is to those who are.

The following story, from Sammy, looks at a conflict

that had existed with Jeremy for some time. Sammy realized that having the opportunity to work through their conflicts is one of the things that allows Pike Place Fish to have such a strong team and to make an impact on people. Recognize how Sammy and Jeremy both committed to Jeremy's success at Pike Place Fish, and how they both learned that letting go of their old thoughts allowed the relationship to begin anew.

I used to get really upset with Jeremy. At first, I would just shut him out; I neglected coaching him. I would use my old style of yelling at him and I validated it by talking with other people about it. I gave him no chance to be great or make the team. The upsets between us had been ongoing. Jim and Johnny had coached me on how to coach Jeremy, prior to this one particular meeting, because at every other meeting we'd spend time talking about our issues. Johnny told me, "You've got to leave Jeremy feeling empowered." Stubborn me was thinking, "What if he just doesn't get it? How many times do I have to tell him?" One day I'd say, "Do it this way," and then the next day I'd have to say it again. I got to the point that I just shut down with Jeremy.

Johnny continued to coach me on coaching Jeremy and said that obviously my interpretation of leaving Jeremy empowered wasn't working. He also spoke to Jeremy on separate occasions. We still didn't have it resolved, so when we got to this one meeting in particular, Johnny said to Jeremy, "What is stopping you from creating a relationship with Sammy and getting what he is trying to tell you?"

Well, Jeremy just spilled his guts. While he was speaking, I was just getting more and more angry. They told me not to say anything until he got all of his thoughts out. He was really upset. So I just sat there listening and getting more and more upset. The whole thing just seemed to be spiraling out of control. It was heavy-duty.

Then when it was my turn, I just said, "He does this and he does that... He... He... He...." Once we both got all of our thoughts out on the table, I realized it was so stupid. Once we had both vented, Jim said to me, "Now, Sam, you have to commit to Jeremy making it here." And then Jeremy had to commit to me *making* him make it here, and the next day our relationship was perfect. Just like that. Isn't that weird? I mean, really. I couldn't believe it myself, and I've been working here for years. Both of us committed to each other for Jeremy to make it.

He agreed that if I say something to him in coaching, he can't say something back. And if I tell him to do something that he has already done, then he has permission — and I have to sit there and listen — when he tells me to shut up [*laughing*]. We agreed that there would be certain times of the day — like when it's really busy — that it may sound like I'm yelling at him, but he just has to under-

Sammy

stand that it's busy and not say anything. We added some appropriateness to the timing of the coaching, and that was it. We agreed that night, at that one meeting, and we agreed to not too many rules and regulations — just one per person. Then we just took it from there.

In addition, everyone else at the meeting agreed to have Jeremy and Sammy have a new relationship; therefore, neither could go to someone else and have their thoughts validated or justified. Since then, Sammy has realized that what happened with Jeremy was great because so many times people carry on bad relationships with their coworkers for years, and they get to a place where they do not even know that they can't let go of it. They can work all the way to retirement being miserable.

There's no room for any opportunity for greatness when you have to expend that mental energy on making someone out to be this, that, or the other, just out of being self-righteous or because you aren't big enough to get it out and see what kind of relationship is possible. Because of the ability to get through even major conflicts like that, we do make an impact out there. It's awesome.

Sammy

How Fast Can You Get Off the Hook?

The fishmongers cannot progress or move forward if they are hooked. "How fast can you get off the hook?" asks how quickly the fishmongers are able to get over a conflict or quit being upset about something. Sometimes they are able to get off the hook on their own, but if it involves another person, then the issue usually needs to be discussed and cleared up with that person. Jaison's story shows how getting off the hook opens up opportunities for a new relationship with another person—a relationship that you may not have imagined before. The faster a fishmonger can get off whatever is hooking him, the faster he will be able to access this new opportunity.

How do I get off the hook? For me, communicating is usually the best way, because I'm holding something in. For example, yesterday I was upset because I had to work on my normal day off and had to cancel plans—I wasn't upset, but I got off to a bad start. I had to get out

Matt and Erik behind the counter

of that negative frame of mind. I know I sometimes let my thoughts control me, instead of
taking charge of my thinking. I'm conscious of
it, so I know that the fastest way for me to get
back on track is to communicate with the customers — or anybody. Just talking with somebody will get me off the hook. I can't be upset
when I am creating relationships with people.

I have to just take a deep breath, not bind
myself up, and reach out somehow. It may be
as simple as just saying "Hi" to somebody. Then
it just goes away. But if I resist the fact that I
am upset or frustrated, I stay in that mode.

Jaison

Most of the fishmongers have learned to transform themselves from ordinary to great. To do that, they have to recognize that "it's all over here." They need to be conscious of their intention. Becoming aware of their intention generally is enough to quickly get them off the hook. The Pike Place Fish culture supports conflict and problems because a new opportunity is always on the horizon. Each of the fishmongers has been taught to resolve problems or conflict on his or her own, without bringing in the cavalry. Thus, the general attitude toward problems is very positive: The bigger the problem, the bigger the opportunity.

Being able to get off the hook quickly is a learned skill that improves with practice; fortunately, life provides lots of opportunity to practice. The following example comes from a meeting when Bugge got hooked on a conversation about who Pike Place Fish was being as a world famous organization. The discussion was about whether or not the monthly financial goal would be reached.

The conversation began with some dialogue about why things were the way they were. Unbeknownst to everyone, however, Bugge became hooked on thinking that *he* was the person responsible. At no time in the conversation was his name specifically mentioned, but in his mind the responsibility was falling on him. As a result, he reacted and got defensive. He got upset, he folded his arms, and his tone of voice and his language changed.

At that moment, because of his commitment to the fishmongers, Johnny seized the opportunity to coach Bugge out of this conflict in front of everyone. He stopped the discussion about the goal and said that there was a problem. He told everyone that Bugge was hooked, and he declared his intention and his commitment to making Bugge the greatest. Then he began to coach Bugge. To set the stage for the coaching, Johnny first asked if Bugge would allow himself to be coached, and Bugge said, "Yes." Then Johnny asked if it was Bugge's intention to be a great manager. Bugge said, "Yes." Then Johnny said, "Who are you being right now?"

That was all it took—Bugge got it. Really got it, right before our eyes. Just that one statement showed Bugge who he was being (via the language and behaviors Bugge was demonstrating), and he was able to compare it with the type of manager that he aspired to be. His demeanor changed immediately, his voice lightened up, and he even smiled. He saw he had hooked himself, and he saw his intention presented to him by Johnny; as a result, Bugge altered who he was being. And that was it; he was transformed as quickly as he had gotten hooked!

The greatest thing about that exchange was that every person sitting at the table benefited from the opportunity, because to some extent other fishmongers besides Bugge were hooked on their thinking and on defensive reactions to not reaching the sales goal. Because the coaching was presented before the group, each person had an opportunity to grow from it, each had a new possibility to be altered or transformed, and each could recommit to the Pike Place Fish vision. At that moment, the concept of "world famous" was very present.

Knowing when a problem has become a new opportunity is really a moot point. If you have to ask whether a transformation has occurred, then chances are it has not. It is like flipping on a light switch; the change is that dramatic, even over the little things. You know when someone gets it — there is not a doubt in your mind or in theirs.

Problems: Doorways to the Future

We have already seen in several stories how problems and conflict can be a direct line to transformation. However, one never knows how the new opportunity will show up. An opportunity is an occurrence that is unpredictable, unexpected, and spontaneous, but it should not be confused with accident or coincidence. An opportunity is a spontaneous phenomenon because one does not know exactly what needs to occur within the problem for the opportunity to become a real breakthrough. An example of this spontaneity is demonstrated in Dicky's story.

> Being the manager of Pike Place Fish has a lot
> to do with coaching and listening. We have
> conflicts or problems from time to time. Being
> committed to the vision at Pike Place Fish is
> hard work. Listening is just tremendous. I have
> to listen from nothing and not be self-righteous
> about any negative thoughts that come up.
> Everybody is going to be upset at some point
> or another — we're human beings and we can't
> help it. When I'm upset, Johnny is usually the
> one that helps me take responsibility for
> things in my life.

My commitment is to transform each of them from ordinary to great. It's a process, and our meetings make us go through a lot of processes because we start every meeting with any upsets that anyone has. For some people, it takes longer than others. We always talk about coaching and allowing yourself to be coached. I can't deal with someone forever if they won't allow themselves to be coached — it's like talking to a wall. I have to make sure that they will allow themselves to be coached before I coach them. It doesn't always work, but my commitment is for each one of these guys to be the greatest.

When there is a problem with one of the fishmongers, I can tell by looking at his or her face. By having my listening and coaching available to them, the fishmongers are usually able to clear up any problems very fast, which is good. It is something unique. The opportunities that come out of the fishmongers' problems are absolutely tremendous. As their coach, I learned I just have to listen and help them find where the problem is.

What they share is usually where the core of the problem is. There are usually layers to the problem, and I help them find it. Sometimes they can't find it. Sometimes it is from way, way back in their past and does not even exist today. It only exists in their mind, but sometimes they aren't even aware that they have that thought they carry from their past. But there is always something that happens today that keys them in to become upset. It's like a trigger, and whenever that trigger hits, they get mad. So that's my part as their manager. I have to listen to all of the problems and conflicts and help them find greatness in themselves.

Dicky

There is no prescription for turning problems into opportunities. However, one of the most interesting things about the process is that the opportunity actually creates a breakthrough to a new view and experience of life. One way this new view can emerge is that constraints from the past disappear, as though the universe is prodding a human being into growth. The fishmongers allow themselves freedom from rationalizing or justifying something that has occurred in their past, and that allows them to break through to a new way of thinking or living — or more accurately, to a new life. Problems are opportunities by which transformation can occur.

Chris tells a story about how he had to get upset over not having enough ice under the clams and mussels before he was reminded of his commitment to the other fishmongers and to the vision of Pike Place Fish.

For the most part, I'm open to coaching. I hear it, take a minute to get it, and I move on. But this particular time, I bought into a conversation that I had created about Bear's coaching. I told myself I knew how to set up my display and did not want or need any coaching. I was going to set up the show my way because I was doing it right; I was not wrong. (Hello, ego!) I was hooked.

The funny thing is that I liked my thinking so well that I wanted to share it with others (ha ha). What better way to validate this than by getting others on board, right? I told Russell that Bear was on my case and it was getting old. To my surprise, Russell called me on it right away. He coached me on being coached. He let me know that Bear only coaches one way, and that's for perfection.

So I took these thoughts, got in the delivery truck, and left to pick up the fish for the day. I got a few blocks from the shop, pulled over, and made a choice. I decided to get off being hooked on my disempowering thinking and changed the way I was dealing with Bear. I had to recognize that Bear is a world-class coach, because I also want perfection in the shop. When I got back to the shop, I told Bear, "I have not allowed myself to be coached by you and that is over." Now I think that Bear is making me the best I can be. I acknowledged him at the next meeting for who he is and what he is to the shop.

The opportunity, Chris realized, was not what he thought it would be. While Chris and Bear had an opportunity to re-create their relationship, the bigger revelation was found in the way Russell handled it. It would have been easy for Russell to agree with Chris's thoughts about Bear, but Russell chose not to agree. By taking it further and coaching Chris on accepting coaching, Russell helped Chris get off the hook. That shows Russell's commitment to Chris.

> I know that we are all committed to each other's success. I had the opportunity to see that, when I didn't take Bear's coaching. When I refused his coaching, I was not *being* my commitment to myself, to the person coaching me, or to the vision of Pike Place Fish.
>
> *Chris*

Something interesting happens when you go through the process of transforming a problem into an opportunity. When you are in the midst of a problem, you may come to a point where you do not know how it will ever work itself out. When you get to where you just don't know the solution to the problem, however, something strange happens: You actually lose your attachment to the outcome. On the other hand, as long as you stay attached to a certain outcome, you cannot allow any solutions or new opportunities to show up.

The most amazing thing about the fishmongers' understanding is that they approach life — and whatever curveballs they are thrown — ready to deal with it in greatness. To be ordinary would be to just accept whatever life offers, but at Pike Place Fish that is not acceptable — an attitude seen in the following story from Doug.

> One day in the shop, one of the fishmongers was being aggressive with customers. I don't mind it if they know them, but when they just come out being obnoxious or sarcastic, that's not cool — especially if they don't know what they're doing. Then Darren did something similar. I got upset because I felt Darren knew better.
>
> It wasn't just Darren; it was me. I thought, "These guys are being ridiculous." That wasn't really what was happening. It was just me getting upset. So I threw a bag of shrimp at Darren kind of hard, out of frustration, and he looked at me and said, "This is called anger management." We both had our own thoughts about what was happening, and we were both wrong. The opportunity to resolve it came at the meeting that night, when Darren chose to acknowledge me. As soon as he said, "I'd like to acknowledge Doug," I knew right then that it was the beginning steps of an opportunity.
>
> We coached each other on how we should speak to each other with respect. For me, I had to acknowledge what I did was wrong — throwing the shrimp. He, in return, automatically

acknowledged his response to me was wrong. We came to an understanding that we probably ought to be more professional and acknowledged that we both want what's best for the company and for each other as individuals. We love each other; we hugged each other, had tears in the eyes — the whole thing. Well, that's what happens when an opportunity presents itself! When we got done with everything, we had a new relationship. It was like, "Wow! This is what we needed!"

It takes courage to do that. It takes courage to apologize and to give the coaching in the right way, because it doesn't always come out in the right way. Having conflicts is awesome. If you see getting upset as "I'm wrong / I'm terrible," which a lot of people do, then finding the opportunity is going to be tough. Or if getting upset means that the ol' ego shows up... All kinds of interesting actions will show up when someone is protecting their ego. The opportunity can only occur when I am willing to put my ego aside and accept my part in the problem.

Doug

The fishmongers recognize that the possibility for something completely new can come from something as common as a problem; therefore, they have changed the way they react to problems in their lives. The fishmongers' lives have actually been altered by a change in their thinking about problems, obstacles, challenges, curveballs — whatever we call them. Consider a problem that you are currently dealing with and how you can create an opportunity from it. You can experience a more powerful life, creating opportunities from problems rather than just allowing them to upset you.

Review of Chapter 6

✳ Most opportunities for transformation come out of a problem or a conflict of some sort.

✳ Conflict occurs when your experience does not match your expectation, when the ego gets in the way, or when "it's all over there."

✳ The bigger the problem, the greater the opportunity for transformation.

7 Live What Inspires You

Expanding Your Focus beyond Yourself

The fishmongers believe that to live what inspires them requires expanding their focus and intention beyond themselves. The first step was for each person to take responsibility for their lives, including their thoughts, their words, and their actions. Once they began to inhabit a realm where "it's all over here," they transformed and expanded their focus beyond Pike Place Fish. Transformation occurred by creating an idea about what they would like to have in their lives and in their organization. Profound things happened when they did, and opportunities began to show up that they never could have imagined. At that moment, transformation was possible.

Anders shares how many people in organizations do not think about making a difference for their customers or clients. Business is simply business. He believes that people spend so much time focusing on making the sale that they lose sight of the person making the purchase. The irony is that focusing on the customer or client will generally lead to the initial desired outcome of making the sale.

> Making a difference for people is something that most businesses don't think about. They focus on putting money in the cash register. I go into a place and there is no eye contact, and people don't talk to me. It's usually all about business, but I want to get more personal. I want people to leave my shop smiling and be a positive influence in their everyday interaction.
> Most people think that getting from point A to point B doesn't matter. People say, "I have to go to the store and buy some fish for my family for dinner." They get so focused on the actual dinner later on — the whole driving to the store, selecting their fish, paying at the register, doing whatever, and getting back to their house — that they aren't even present. They're missing it. They're just preplanning for this dinner and living in this future that is hours away. In the meantime, two hours of their life is gone. I want to fill in those gaps with good stuff, with good interaction. All the so-called "little things in between" *are* life.

> *Anders*

Taking responsibility for the goals at the Market and for what shows up has made an incredible impact in Anders's life. He sometimes gets frustrated with the unawareness of people, how everyone is a victim, and how it is always "over there." He wonders how people can go through life seemingly asleep. At the same time, Anders recognizes that he cannot get frustrated at those people just because they are not aware. He believes his job, as someone who wants to make a difference, is to make them aware and to wake them up, instead of getting frustrated.

The fishmongers take active responsibility for the outcomes they experience, by expanding their focus beyond themselves. When you are more focused on making a difference for others than on yourself, you have no idea what will happen. Those are the moments that something really great usually happens to you — without you really trying for it. It is difficult to describe, but when you experience it in your life, you know it. We call those times "divine intervention," "luck," "coincidence," or "fate"; but it is really *you*.

The following story from Jaison demonstrates how having fun at work is great, but that there has to be a lot more to it than just having fun. He believes that fun does not happen without expanding his focus beyond himself and making a difference for others.

> I love when people come up to me at the fish market and say, "Yeah, we throw stuffed fish at work." I think that's a good place to start with coworkers. Everybody should be able to work at a place where it is enjoyable and there's no

stagnation — where it is alive. But from there, I have to go out and share it with the people that I am in contact with. If I just keep it to myself and my coworkers, then it doesn't get out there and make a difference for anyone else. I have to expand my focus beyond myself and the people I work with.

When I think about how I share with customers or people visiting the shop, it is the way that people smile and the way their faces light up when we interact. The interaction with me is not just buying fish or a business transaction. I know, in retail, making a difference is measured with return customers. I may not have remembered their name, but they've remembered me — Jaison, the musician, the drummer. They'll remember this instance or conversation we had, but when I really touch somebody I create a relationship that lasts over time. How it looks is return customers who want to talk to me. They want my service again.

Jaison

Generating Greatness

Generating greatness at Pike Place Fish is evident in the level of commitment to the success of each fishmonger and in the commitment to making a difference for other people. In the following story, Chris explains how generating greatness means that people can sense he truly cares about them and is willing to go the extra step to make sure that they get the World Famous Pike Place Fish experience. Generating greatness requires a constant loop of communication between the fishmongers. Chris recognizes that at Pike Place Fish he is fortunate enough to get continuous feedback on how he is doing, rather than having to wait for a performance review to learn of his contribution.

> I was somewhat aware of what to expect at the fish market because I was friends with a couple of the guys. I was conscious that there was a lot more than just throwing fish around and a lot of hollering. Making a difference for people was something I had never expected. Customers could just as easily go to other fish stands as they could come to ours. But they choose to come here because of who I am being with them. They sense I truly care about them and I will go the extra step with them. It's more than just fish.
>
> Each of us contributes differently to the overall picture. I'm more reserved than some of the others — the behind-the-scenes type. I think of an analogy of a rock-and-roll band. There are lead singers that are up in front, drum players keeping the beat going in the back, and I'm like the bass player: kind of quiet but keeping the melody going. I keep the cooler stocked and do all my side work, making sure

the people that are the rock stars can do what they need to do. That's my contribution.

It's unusual because some people can work for a company for five years or more and never know how their contributions are viewed or know if they are part of anything. At some companies, you have to wait for your performance appraisal to find out how you're doing. Here at Pike Place Fish, I get immediate feedback because I am coaching and being coached constantly.

If I do something that is not aligned to the vision of being world famous or to our quality of service or product, somebody will let me know right then. It's also my responsibility to tell somebody when I notice it in someone else. It doesn't matter if I've been here for a week or ten years, I am responsible for everyone. Everyone is responsible for each other and dedicated to Pike Place Fish being great and touching people's lives.

Chris

In generating greatness, the fishmongers have come to see that situations and circumstances are not nearly as solid as they first appear. In fact, circumstances are far more malleable than one may ever realize, and in expanding the focus beyond Pike Place Fish, the fishmongers have discovered that they are far more powerful than they ever imagined.

Generating greatness is a process of being aware of intentions and being committed to making it happen. The fishmongers may not always know what or how it will happen, just that it will. For each person, generating greatness means something different. In Bison's story, greatness means cleaning out the cooler — making many fish fly!

The one thing that I could tell people, as far as transforming an organization to make a difference, is that I live for whatever inspires me. I create games with myself. When I'm up top I try to ring the most sales. If I'm the grunt for the day then I don't expect to ring as much because I'm doing the back room and doing the buckets at the end of the night. Other than that, if I'm not close to the top guy I'm upset, and it makes me work harder. Depending on the circumstances, I drive myself and challenge myself in all that I do. I try to clean the cooler out as much as I can in terms of getting rid of all the fish.

I'm competitive with myself and my team in a positive way, but not at the cost of someone else's performance. If each of us is striving to be the best, it will make an ordinary company great. If we expand our performance to include the performance of the whole organization, it makes work more enjoyable. Even if I am not the biggest seller, I challenge myself to do more. I try new things, like working on my filleting or packing/shipping technique to master them. Then I'll go out in front and master that. But I always have the other crewmembers on my mind as well as my own performance.

I love the Pike Place way of life. It puts things in a very clear-cut understanding of how people should take it and apply it. The best part is that the ideas can be translated to any type of business. If you sell insurance and you specialize in car insurance, then become an expert in home insurance or something else. Master your customer service skills; master the way that you deal with coworkers. I do whatever I can to make myself more valuable to the team or the company, without taking away from someone else in the company. It can be easy to outperform my coworkers when all I care about is myself, but it is a different story when my performance increases and I am able to increase the performance of my coworkers as well. *That* is generating greatness!

Bison

An important point in Bison's story is that greatness can never come at the cost of someone else's greatness. True greatness comes when it is generated in others as well. Greatness is not a result of what the fishmongers do individually; it is a result of who they are collectively.

There is no ten-step process to get there because greatness is dependent on each individual and on his or her intention.

To call forth an opportunity for greatness, the fishmongers simply ask themselves who they are being in relation to any given situation, and they find opportunities for greatness all around them. Remember: It's all over here. What does greatness mean to you?

Transformation Begins Now

Generating greatness and finding what inspires you will be unique to you. As Bison showed, generating greatness comes from living and doing whatever inspires him. He generates greatness by working toward mastering all the different operations and areas of Pike Place Fish. In the next story, told by Darren, note that what inspires him is an intention to avoid wasting time, to be very present in his life.

> One thing that Pike Place Fish has taught me is how to stay present in my life. As a result, I don't waste my time anymore. I don't waste my time with people who will waste my time or with situations that will waste my time. Time is precious, so if I'm in a relationship, a friendship, or a situation with someone that isn't working for me, or if it's not exactly what I want to be doing in that certain time, I don't do it. There are things that I have to do and

there are things that I just do because I feel obligated for whatever reason. I just don't do it anymore.

This isn't to be confused with being selfish. I have to take care of myself before I can take care of other people. A big part of my life is taking care of other people — friends, my comrades, and coworkers. I want to nurture them, take care of them, and do things for them. And I do.

Working at Pike Place Fish has made me very conscious of how my life affects other people. I always ask myself if I'm living my life for myself or am I being available in every way that I can in my life to make a difference in another human being? It's a matter of being conscious and always being in the present, so I can be available for others in any way I can.

Darren

The fishmongers have come to realize, like Darren, how precious time is. They also realize how precious relationships are. It has been said in many of these stories that generating greatness — creating new opportunities, being aware of thinking and language — is a lifestyle. It is an evolutionary process and is based on the fundamental belief that you create what you experience in your life. Greatness is dependent on how you communicate with others, and more powerfully, on how you communicate with yourself. As Anders relates, you must recognize the power you have as an individual.

> If my intention is that I want our customers to know that I am here to make them happy, then when someone is genuinely unhappy, I stop and let them know that I am committed to them leaving my shop smiling. I'll tell them, "I want you to leave happy and I'll do whatever it takes to make that happen." For example, with this one guy I said, "You're upset. I understand you're upset, but things happen. We're human beings. What will it take for you to leave Pike Place Fish happy and want to come back?" He had been acting very cold, and it kind of broke his guard down.
>
> He said, "Having heard that... Well, I guess I could get another crab." After a few seconds, his whole demeanor changed and he almost felt silly for acting that way. That was all I could do for him. He had been attached to whatever was upsetting him. I made him real-ize how simple a thing it was. I made his experience work for him, and he left happy.
>
> There are still going to be some people who aren't going to leave my shop happy, and all I can do for those people is hope that who I was being when I interacted with them is going to make them realize it. It's my intention, and

attention to our vision at Pike Place Fish, that gives me the power to change someone's bad day or bad attitude into a positive one.

People say that they can't make a difference in their company because they are just one person, and their company has hundreds, or thousands, or hundreds of thousands of employees. Get this: I am one-seventeenth of Pike Place Fish, and we have made a difference in literally millions of people's lives. If you break that up, those millions of people, and divide them by seventeen, I'm responsible for all those people, and I am just one person. You are only as insignificant as you say you are.

Look at all these people who have changed the world, all these "one-persons" who generated greatness. Martin Luther King, Jr., Nelson Mandela, Gandhi, and FDR — each of them was only one person. If they had felt like they were a part of a system that they had no control of, they wouldn't have changed the world in the ways that they have — and continue to. If I said that I was insignificant and couldn't transform my organization, I would be right — but only because I said so, not because that is the reality, because it is not.

Anders

We do not live on a static planet. It is dynamic, evolving, and changing on every level, every day and every year.

Russell and Matt with a happy customer

What makes our era unique is the rate of transformation that we are experiencing today. Change occurs at a faster rate today than in former times, and sometimes it is difficult to keep up. Our entire lives are a process of transformation on several levels — physical, emotional, intellectual, and spiritual. No one is exempt from this process we call life.

More than ever, we want the fullest experience we can get out of life in the short amount of time we're here — all of which requires a shift in thinking and a new way of being. The fishmongers at Pike Place Fish have opened themselves to their intentions, as well as to their generative and creative nature.

The most important thing to remember is that transformation begins with you, exactly as you are right now.

Whatever results you experience with this book are up to you; however, if you are willing, it is the intention of Pike Place Fish that this book will enable you to create new and powerful opportunities for yourself, your relationships, your workplace, your communities, and your world.

Through the fishmongers' stories, you may gather a new way of thinking that allows you to become more effective in your life and your work. As you explore these concepts in your life, you may see your life alter. Things may change around you, so recognize that it is you who is creating the change, who is creating those opportunities. Go forth into the world of infinite possibilities, living powerfully, being responsible for your experience, and generating greatness in your life.

Review of Chapter 7

✳ You will generate greatness when you start expanding your focus and intention beyond yourself.

✳ Fun does not happen without a commitment to making a difference for other people.

✳ Greatness cannot come at the cost of someone else's performance.

✳ Transformation begins with you, exactly as you are.

Index

Page numbers in *italic* type refer to photographs.

Bugge, Dan, 6, *6*, 58–60,
    82–85, 102, 111–112

catch
    the "catch," 15, 33
    customer catching fish,
        11, 39
    See also throwing fish
change
    in thinking, 77, 79,
        89–90, 91–93, 95–96,
        104, 105
    changing the world, 134
    See also making a
        difference;
        transformation
choice
    to be upset, x, 25–26,
        27, 93
    to change, 91–93
    of experience, 24–28
    to have fun, 27–28, 39–
        41, 42–43, 49, 52, 66
    intention and, 42–43,
        45–46, 48–49
    to make a difference,
        31–32, 49
    opportunities and,
        64–69
    outcome and, 57

See also responsibility
Chris Bell, *6*, 6–7, 16–18,
    30–32, 115–117,
    126–128
client. *See* customer
coaching
    to help one another, 60,
        90–91, 128
    management and, 24,
        105, 112, 113–114
    resistance to, 83, 115–117
    to solve problems,
        100–101, 105–108,
        118–119
commitment
    to greatness, 35, 36, 50,
        99–100
    to intention, 35–42, 46,
        47–48, 49, 51, 54
    to making a difference,
        23, 50, 57, 58–60, 126
    to one another, 67,
        99–100, 107, 115, 117
    to opportunity, 64
    to Pike Place Fish, 23,
        28, 29–30
    to transformation, 20
communication. *See*
    coaching; language;
    listening

conflict. *See* problems

cross training, 9

customers
catching fish, 11, 39
happy customers, 18, 39,
40–41, *135*
focusing on customers,
18, 123–124, 133–134,
140
impacting customers,
57–60, 126–127,
133–134
unhappy customers,
57–60, 133–134

Darren Kilian, *5*, 5–6,
21–22, 25–26, 118,
131–132
Dave Brooks, 87–88
Dehn, Ryan ("Bison"), *7*,
7–8, 39–41, 62–63,
89–91, 129–130, 131
Dicky Yokoyama, 3, *4*,
19–21, 103–104, 105,
113–115
difference. *See* making a
difference
doing
and being, 18–20, 21, 22
See also actions

Doug Straus, 8, 27–28,
69–71, 85–87, 118–119

emotions
awareness of, 21
responsibility for, x
See also anger;
happiness; upset
feelings
Erik Espinoza, *6*, 7, 92–93
Espinoza, Erik, *6*, 7, 92–93
experience
as a choice, 24–28
language and, 82, 85, 87,
88
responsibility for, 16, 69,
136
thoughts and, 76, 80, 85,
86–87, 91

fishmongers
defined, viii
introduced, 3–9
Frigulietti, Andy, *6*, 7,
36–37, *37*, 92
fun
as a choice, 27–28,
39–41, 42–43, 49, 52
and making a
difference, 58, 60, 125

fun, *continued*
opportunities for, 60,
66, 69–71
See also happiness

goals
for the day, 9, 11–12
See also intention
greatness
as a choice, 45–46
collective nature of, 130
commitment to, 35, 36,
50, 99–100
generating, 15–16, 105,
126–131, 136
opportunities for, 62,
64, 68, 131
transformation to,
20–21, 23–24, 27, 30,
37–38, 76, 80, 114

Hall, Justin, 3–4, *4*, 48–49,
65–66, 83–84, 101–102
happiness, x, 25, 70, 93
of customer, 133–134
See also fun
happy customers, 18, 39,
40–41, *135*
having, 19. *See also*
outcomes

"hooked," 79–80, 82, 103,
105, 109–112, 116

illness
as opportunity, 69–71
as powerful experience,
51–54, 87–88
integrity, 20, 22, 54
intention
choice and, 42–43,
45–46, 48–49
commitment to, 35–42,
46, 47–48, 49, 51, 54
expansion of, 50–51, 123
importance of, 16, 20,
21, 24, 30–31
opportunities and, 41,
64, 67, 68, 72
outcome and, 39, 41–42,
58
problems and, 69, 94,
105, 111
relationships and, 35,
36–37, 39–41, 43–45,
47
"It's all over here," x, 16, 25,
58, 61, 81, 89–90, 111
relationships and, 100,
102, 103

thoughts, *continued*
   changes in, 77, 79,
      89–90, 91–93, 95–96,
      104, 105
   choice of, 92–93
   experience and, 76, 80,
      85, 86–87, 91
   getting hooked on,
      79–80, 82, 103, 116
   negative, 78, 80, 82, 93,
      105
   power of, 53, 64, 76–79,
      80–81
   reality and, 26, 75, 81, 91
   relationships and, 82,
      103–104, 106
   responsibility for, x, 30,
      76, 87, 90, 103–104
throwing fish, vii, viii, 11,
      15, 23, 49, 67
   into baby carriage, 6
   to customers, 11, 39
   Guinness record, 4
   for tour bus, 66
time, value of, 131–132
transformation
   begins with you,
      135–136
   of being, 25
   beyond yourself, 123

to greatness, 20–21,
   23–24, 27, 30, 37–38,
   76, 80, 114
opportunities for, 99,
   113–115
rate of, in today's world,
   135
thoughts and, 76, 79,
   80, 90, 105
willingness and, 28, 30,
   78
See also making a
   difference

unhappy customers,
   57–60, 133–134
"up on top," 8, 9
upset feelings
   as a choice, x, 25–26, 27,
      93
   communicating about,
      26, 106–107, 109–110,
      114–115
   of customer, 58, 133
   as opportunity for
      growth, 32, 103, 119
   taking responsibility
      for, 101–102, 104, 113
   transformation of, 79
See also anger

willingness, 28, 30, 77–78

work, meaning of, 27–28

"world famous," 17, 19, 23, 28, 41–42, 46, 112

World Famous Pike Place Fish Market. *See* Pike Place Fish

world peace, 30, 140

Yokoyama, Dicky, 3, *4,* 19–21, 103–104, 105, 113–115

Yokoyama, John (Johnny), vii, viii, 3, 20, 29, 47–48, 52, 94, 106–107, 111–112, 113

About the Authors

DR. CYNDI CROTHER

Cyndi Crother is an assis-
tant professor in the In-
dustrial Technology De-
partment at California
Polytechnic State Univer-
sity, San Luis Obispo. For
the past nine years, she

has taught in the areas of quality assurance, corporate
training, teambuilding, management presentations, and
facilities management. As a student of organizational ef-
fectiveness and continuous improvement, Cyndi plans to
write more books about different types of extraordinary
organizations. She is currently working on two more business books and has started a consulting company called
"Guide to Greatness," working with organizations on
change management, leadership development, and systems thinking.

For more information, please contact:

> Dr. Cyndi Crother
> P. O. Box 4344
> San Luis Obispo, CA 93403
> www.guidetogreatness.com
> Cyndi@guidetogreatness.com
> ccrother@calpoly.edu

A few years ago, the crew of Pike Place Fish committed to becoming world famous, and they accomplished this by being truly great with people. Throwing fish has become a highlight of the Pike Place Public Market, and the crew maintains a strong desire to make a difference for people through their interactions. They want to give each person the experience of having been served and appreciated. The crew also stands for the possibility of world peace and of prosperity for all people. They believe that it is possible for one person to affect the way other people experience life. Through their work, they have improved the quality of life for millions of people. They are committed to this belief — it is what they do.

Many businesses and organizations request that the crew and their partner bizFUTURES Consulting offer coaching and instruction on the underlying principles that have shaped Pike Place Fish's success. For more information, please contact:

World Famous Pike Place Fish
86 Pike Place
Seattle, WA 98101
Telephone: 206-682-7181
Toll-free: 1-800-542-7732
Fax: 206-682-4629
pikeplacefish@pikeplacefish.com

Berrett-Koehler Publishers

Berrett-Koehler is an independent publisher of books and other publications at the leading edge of new thinking and innovative practice on work, business, management, leadership, stewardship, career development, human resources, entrepreneurship, and global sustainability.

Since the company's founding in 1992, we have been committed to creating a world that works for all by publishing books that help us to integrate our values with our work and work lives, and to create more humane and effective organizations.

We have chosen to focus on the areas of work, business, and organizations, because these are central elements in many people's lives today. Furthermore, the work world is going through tumultuous changes, from the decline of job security to the rise of new structures for organizing people and work. We believe that change is needed at all levels—individual, organizational, community, and global—and our publications address each of these levels.

To find out about our new books,
special offers,
free excerpts,
and much more,
subscribe to our free monthly eNewsletter at
www.bkconnection.com

Please see next pages for other books
from Berrett-Koehler Publishers

More books from Berrett-Koehler Publishers

628

Fun Works
Creating Places Where People Love to Work

Leslie Yerkes

Leslie Yerkes provides proven tools to unleash the power of fun and make the workplace a winning experience for workers, clients, customers, vendors, and stakeholders alike. It provides a comprehensive set of guiding principles any organization can apply to increase satisfaction and meaning at work by accessing the life-giving force of fun.

Paperback • ISBN 1-57675-154-6 • Item #51546 $18.95

Positively M. A. D.

Edited by Bill Treasurer

Written by more than 50 of Berrett-Koehler's renowned authors, *Positively M. A. D.* is a collection of stories that will inspire readers to take action in their own lives to make a difference in their organizations and communities. These engaging, optimistic, "can do" vignettes are about real people making real changes despite the harsh realities of the modern world.

Paperback • ISBN 1-57675-312-3 • Item #53123 $12.00

Leadership and Self-Deception
Getting Out of the Box

The Arbinger Institute

Leadership and Self-Deception reveals that there are only two ways for leaders to be: the source of leadership problems or the source of leadership success. The authors examine this surprising truth, identify self-deception as the underlying cause of leadership failure, and show how any leader can overcome self-deception to become a consistent catalyst of success.

Hardcover • ISBN 1-57675-094-9 • Item #50949 $22.00
Paperback • ISBN 1-57675-174-0 • Item #51740 $14.95

Berrett-Koehler Publishers
PO Box 565, Williston, VT 05495-9900
Call toll-free! **800-929-2929** 7 am-9 pm EST

Or fax your order to 1-802-864-7626
For fastest service order online: **www.bkconnection.com**

Change Your Questions, Change Your Life
7 Powerful Tools for Life and Work
Marilee G. Adams, Ph.D.

Change Your Questions, Change Your Life introduces QuestionThinking™, a revolutionary yet practical technique you can use to transform your life—simply by learning to ask the right questions of yourself and others.

Paperback • ISBN 1-57675-241-0 • Item #52410 $14.95

Full Steam Ahead!
Unleash the Power of Vision in Your Company and Your Life
Ken Blanchard and Jesse Stoner

Blanchard and Stoner detail the essential elements of creating a successful vision. In *Full Steam Ahead!* you'll learn to use the power of vision to get focused, get energized, and get great results; create a vision that touches the hearts and spirits of everyone in your organization; and create a vision for your own life that provides meaning and direction.

Hardcover • ISBN 1-57675-244-5 • Item #52445 $19.95
Paperback • ISBN 1-57675-306-9 • Item #53069 $14.95

The Secret
Discover What Great Leaders Know —and Do
Ken Blanchard and Mark Miller
Foreword by John C. Maxwell

In *The Secret*, Blanchard and Miller use the uniquely accessible "business fable" format that Blanchard pioneered to get at the heart of what makes a leader truly able to inspire and motivate people.

Hardcover • ISBN 1-57675-289-5 • Item #52895 $19.95

Berrett-Koehler Publishers
PO Box 565, Williston, VT 05495-9900
Call toll-free! **800-929-2929** 7 am-9 pm EST

Or fax your order to 1-802-864-7626
For fastest service order online: **www.bkconnection.com**

Spread the word!

Berrett-Koehler books are available at quantity discounts for orders of 10 or more copies.

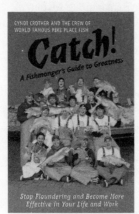

Catch!
A Fishmonger's Guide to Greatness

Cyndi Crother and the Crew of World Famous Pike Place Fish

Paperback, 200 pages
ISBN 978-1-57675-323-1
Item #53231 $14.95

To find out about discounts for orders of 10 or more copies for individuals, corporations, institutions, and organizations, please call us toll-free at (800) 929-2929.

To find out about our discount programs for resellers, please contact our Special Sales department at (415) 288-0260; Fax: (415) 362-2512. Or email us at bkpub@bkpub.com.

Subscribe to our free e-newsletter!

To find out about what's happening at Berrett-Koehler and to receive announcements of our new books, special offers, free excerpts, and much more, subscribe to our free monthly e-newsletter at www.bkconnection.com.

Berrett-Koehler Publishers
PO Box 565, Williston, VT 05495-9900
Call toll-free! **800-929-2929** 7 am-9 pm EST

Or fax your order to 1-802-864-7626
For fastest service order online: **www.bkconnection.com**